"For thousands of years men have speculated about the nature of
human consciousness. Only within the last fifty years, however, scientists gained the technical ability to describe the physiological and
biochemical correlates of states of consciousness. This ability has
enabled them to better understand the processes and neural structures
which underlie these states." (R. K. Wallace, "The Physiological
Effects of Transcendental Meditation--A Proposed Fourth State of Consciousness," Ph.D. Theses, UCLA, 1970)

"When you speak of 'consciousness', you do not refer to the moral
conscious: the very rigor of your methods ensures that you do not
leave the strictly scientific domain which belongs to you. What you
have in mind exclusively is the faculty of perceiving and of reacting
to perception, that is to say, the psychophysiological concept which
constitutes one of the accepted meanings of the word 'consciousness.'
(Pope Paul VI addressing a gathering of Scientists for the study of
Brain and Conscious Experience, Rome 1964).

The level of consciousness is determined by "the degree of one's
ability to utilize the past and contribute to the future. Consciousness is usually defined by the ability (1) to appreciate sensory information; (2) to react critically to it with thoughts or movements
(actions); (3) to permit the accumulation of memory traces. So during
(deep) sleep we have either no consciousness at all or (during dreaming)
a very low level of consciousness." (N. Kleitman, Sleep and Wakefulness,
U. of Chicago Press, 1963).

THE PSYCHOBIOLOGY OF TRANSCENDENTAL MEDITATION

A Literature Review

By
Demetri P. Kanellakos
Jerome S. Lukas

W. A. Benjamin, Inc.
Menlo Park, California. Reading, Massachusetts. London.
Amsterdam. Don Mills, Ontario. Sydney

Library of Congress Catalog No. 74-7524

ISBN 0-8053-5205-8

ISBN 0-8053-5205-8
ABCDEFGHIJ-AL-7987654

PREFACE

This book incorporates a Final Report of a research program funded by the Stanford Research Institute (SRI), Menlo Park, California. The purpose of this program was (1) to prepare a literature survey of the physiological and psychological effects of Transcendental Meditation (TM), (2) to carry out a pilot study to determine the teachability of the TM technique to a non-predisposed section of the population (in this case SRI staff members), and (3) to replicate some of the findings of investigative studies on meditators that have been reported in the literature.

In the past four years, Transcendental Meditation (TM) has been the subject of more research than any of the other meditative techniques, and yet there has been no literature survey on the psychophysiology of TM as there have been for other forms of meditation. For those two reasons we devote this review almost exclusively to research and literature on TM.

The pioneer paper on the physiological effects of TM first published by Robert Keith Wallace in Science, 1970 is a summary of his Ph.D dissertation in Physiology at the University of California, Los Angeles, and is based upon work supported by a grant from the U. S. Public Health Service. Shortly after the publication of this paper and Wallace's book containing his full thesis (1970), many investigators attempted to verify his findings, and research on TM rapidly expanded in a number of areas, particularly psychology and medicine. This early research was surveyed as part of the SRI study, and much of it is summarized in the original SRI report published in February, 1973*. This report is on pages 3-54.

In response to the large number of requests for the original report, permission was granted to the authors to publish independently an updated version with W. A. Benjamin, Inc. so that the very latest investigative findings on TM could be more accessible. This new version reviews the published and unpublished research literature up to about January, 1974. References to and abstracts of theoretical articles about TM have been included, as well as some on other forms of meditation. Additional references are given to selected popular or nontechnical articles and books, primarily on TM. And again a selection of publications on other techniques is included, because what is presented on TM may be applicable to many, or all other, meditative practices.

---

*Final Report: The Psychobiology of Transcendental Meditation: A Literature Review; IR&D Project 933535 - AFB, February, 1973

No attempt has been made to integrate or interpret the findings reported, for their reliability is not fully established. Our purpose has simply been to present the available data so that it may be clearly understood by those readers not specifically qualified in the areas of biology and psychology.

Finally we wish to specifically note the recent expansion of scientific interest in TM. Since Wallace published his first paper in 1970, the number of laboratories studying the psychobiological effects of TM has grown from 4 to over 100 as of this writing. Over 70 of these are in the United States. This scientific effort to investigate TM, and to compare its practice and its effects with those of other meditative techniques, should continue to grow as more and more people take up the practice of meditation. For TM alone, the number of TM practitioners is reported to exceed 360,000, as of May, 1974, just in the United States.*

D. P. Kanellakos
J. S. Lukas
July 1974

*Source: Students International Meditation Society (SIMS); headquarters, 1015 Gayley Street, Los Angeles, California 90024. (Approximately 15,000 persons a month are now being instructed in this practice.)

CONTENTS

ILLUSTRATIONS

TABLES

ILLUSTRATIONS

1. [illegible]

2. [illegible]

3. [illegible]

4. [illegible]

5. [illegible]

6. [illegible]

7. [illegible]

8. [illegible]

9. [illegible]

10. [illegible]

11. [illegible]

TABLES

1. [illegible]

2. [illegible]

3. [illegible]

FOREWORD

Transcendental Meditation (TM) is a special type of meditative technique developed by Maharishi Mahesh Yogi (1966, 1969)* that involves sitting quietly with the eyes closed for 15-20 minutes daily before morning and evening meals and allowing the mind to think a special thought without effort. Its practitioners purport that TM induces a wakeful state of deep relaxation, certain concomitant physiological and biological changes, and that it influences behavioral changes in the practitioner outside of the meditative state. The state of wakeful relaxation induced during TM is called the Transcendental State or TC state. Adherents of TM claim that the TC state constitutes a state of human consciousness which is distinct from the three currently recognized states of wakefulness, deep sleep, and dreaming.

Is there a "transcendental state?" If there is, how can it be identified? How does it relate to the other more commonly recognized states of consciousness? The subject matter of this book is directed toward finding the answers to these questions. We have adopted the general approach of emphasizing and describing the physiological differences between the hypothesized TC-state and the three recognized major states of consciousness.

A. The relationship of the TC-state to the other three major states of consciousness.

An initial understanding of the meditative or transcendental state may be facilitated by showing its relationships to the three other major states of consciousness. Below is a highly schematized and simplified illustration of some of the possible relationships between these major states.

Level of Physiological Activity

	High	Low	
Relative Sensitivity to Internal Stimuli (Low/High)	Awake	Transcendent	Relative Sensitivity to External Stimuli (High/Low)
	Dreaming	Deep Sleep	

---

* References cited in the text are listed on pp. 49-54.

It must be understood that various physiological and psychological parameters always vary along some continuum and that, for any given individual, although his psychological or physiological state is relatively "normal" from day to day, actual measurements of various physiological or psychological parameters may indicate the individual to be more or less "normal" for that day as compared to other days. With reference to the diagram, therefore, the scientific task becomes one of establishing the limits that indicate unequivocally (or define) that the individual is in one state or another. For example, the diagram shown above suggests that, with respect to external stimuli, an individual may show a greater or a lesser degree of receptivity and awareness depending upon whether he is awake or asleep -- e.g., upon his state of consciousness. However, the absolute intensity of a particular stimulus required to establish unequivocally that the individual is awake or asleep is yet to be measured. Of course, the electroencephalogram and other physiological measures provide a fairly reliable differentiation between wakefulness and sleep. But the electroencephalographic patterns which clearly indicate that the subject is transcending are by no means fully established. Thus, the rationale for assembling this review was to select and group those research papers which dealt with particular physiological or psychological variables that, in our opinion, permit reasonably reliable differentiation between the states of consciousness.

In some cases, the experiments reported herein were preliminary in nature and lacked conventional scientific rigor. At times, adequate controls were omitted, the number of subjects used was small, the criteria used for subject selection were not stated (e.g., in experiments using TM practitioners, the length of time the subjects has been practicing TM was not always reported), and sometimes the data were not analyzed statistically.

But a reasonable proportion of the data are sufficiently "hard" and promising so as to warrant more systematic research in this area. Especially noteworthy is the fact that most of the data illustrate trends which appear to be consistent from experiment to experiment. These trends point to physiological effects that are consistent with deep relaxation, reduced reactivity, and to psychological effects that include greater self-actualization, an enhanced self-image, and greater "peace" within oneself. We have not attempted to compare TM with so-called "altered states of consciousness" such as those induced by drugs, hypnosis, autogenic training, and other relaxation techniques. But whenever the opportunity presented itself, however, we did compare changes in psychobiological variables reported for TM with those reported for wakefulness, sleep and dreaming, since TM appears to relate to these states in some as-yet-unspecified way.

Future research is needed to test the reliability of this work on the presumed TC-state and the significance of the many anecdotal claims regarding the amelioration or reversal of a wide variety of physical and behavioral complaints of deviations, including drug abuse. This book should provide some direction to that research.

B. Structure of this Book

This book is divided into several major sections and appendices. Section I provides background information that led to this review. The review begins in Section II (pp. 3-22. Here we deal with the more important physiological correlates of wakefulness, deep sleep, and dreaming, and we compare them with those of the suggested state of transcendental consciousness (TC). Additional correlates of the TC-state may be found in Appendix A.

Section III (pp. 23-27) deals with the psychological effects of TM Practice, including its apparent beneficial effect on the drug abuse problem, improved reaction time, more stable autonomic nervous system functioning, better auditory and visual perception, improved general psychological and mental health bringing about imporved creativity. More data on these subjects plus beginnings of certain medical applications of TM on asthma, insomnia, dream "rebound," high blood pressure, reduced gum inflammation, and reduced anxiety and tension in prisoners can be found in the abstracts of Appendix A.

In Section IV (pp. 39-45) we deal briefly with the question of whether there are any deleterious effects resulting from the practice of TM. We are grateful for the comments offered by Maharishi Mahesh Yogi on this problem.

Appendix A (pp. 57-120) is an annotated bibliography of published papers as well as many unpublished reports (such as Ph.D. and Master's theses and the findings of pilot studies). The first part (pp. 57-94) covers material on the physiology and psychology of TM, followed by the second part (pp. 97-120) which deals with TM and drug abuse. The third, fourth, fifth and sixth parts include material on the theory of TM and altered states of consciousness (pp. 102-109), the psychophysiology of other meditation techniques (pp. 109-113), and the psychobiology of wakefulness, deep sleep and dreaming (pp. 113-115) and biofeedback, yoga, and other exercises (pp. 115-120). Part seven (pp. 120) of Appendix A deals with research coordination.

Appendix B describes the steps required to learn TM. However, the reader is cautioned that to obtain optimum results he should seek a qualified TM teacher through a SIMS center. He should not attempt to learn TM by himself.

Appendix C contains some testimonials of TM practitioners. Such material is sometimes useful in designing psychological and physiological test measures and procedures.

Appendix D contains certain articles that have appeared in popular magazines and some scientific papers and reports that are not included in Appendix A.

We conclude with an epilogue by Dr. Hans Seyle of Montreal University. Dr. Seyle, a noted authority on the biological stress syndrome, makes a personal statement on the effects of the development of consciousness in humans and points out the necessary course of research on TM and related topics one must know in order to understand the somatic (hormonal) changes induced by the practice of meditation.

ACKNOWLEDGMENTS

We wish to express our gratitude to those individuals who are doing research on various aspects of TM and who supplied us with advance copies of their research designs and preliminary findings so that they could be included in this report. It is hoped that our presentation of these reports does the authors' work justice and does not distort the final results of the research.

An epilogue prepared by Dr. Hans Selye, pioneer in stress research at the Institute of Experimental Medicine and Surgery, University of Montreal, Montreal, Canada, makes a meaningful distinction between "stress" and "distress" and introduces the term "eustress". We thank him for his contribution to our effort.

We are particularly grateful to Maharishi Mahesh Yogi for certain of the explanatory material he has offered for Chapter V regarding the present understanding of the nature of meditation and its possible deleterious effects in the modern way of life.

Our thanks, also, to the various publishers and authors cited in the text, bibliography or appendices for their permission to reproduce figures or quote from their papers.

I INTRODUCTION

The three major recognized states of the organism for which relatively unambiguous psychobiological correlates have been identified are the state of wakefulness, the state of deep sleep,* and the dreaming state (Kleitman, 1963; Dement, 1958, 1964). For each of these major states, a different set of physiological and biochemical conditions exists, although there is some overlap of the conditions among the states. During wakefulness, the central nervous system and somatic functioning are geared toward voluntary thought and action. During deep sleep, physiological and biochemical processes take place that apparently prepare the human body for physiological functioning during wakefulness. Luce (1965, 1970) and Hartman (1973) have suggested that processes take place during dreaming that apparently facilitate rational functioning during wakefulness.

It has been hypothesized (Maharishi Mahesh Yogi, 1966, 1969; Deikman, 1963, 1966 a,b) that the nervous system may also manifest a fourth major state -- the "transcendental state" (or "TC-state"),** induced by meditation. The physiological processes that take place during the time the human nervous system is in the TC-state are thought to relieve the strains and stresses that have accumulated in the human nervous system and that are not relieved by sleep or dreaming.

Before describing the physiological and psychological correlates of meditation, however, a brief discussion of meditation itself may be helpful to some readers.

It must be understood initially that at present there is no single, commonly accepted technique for meditating or for attaining the meditative ("transcendental" may be synonymous) state, although most techniques require the meditator to sit quietly with a relaxed posture. Differing details of the various techniques range from simple contemplation or visualization of an object, such as a vase, or a sound (a mantra,*** as in transcendental

---

* There are two states (1 and 2) of sleep that apparently are intermediate between wakefulness and "deep" sleep (Sleep Stages 3 and 4).
** Twenty altered states of consciousness have been proposed by Kripner (1972). Five major states of consciousness have been suggested by Walker (1964), Wescott (1969), and de Ropp (1968). Seven major states of consciousness are discussed by Maharishi Mahesh Yogi (1969), Campbell (1974) and Kanellakos (in White, 1974 c).
***A Mantra is a specific sound.

meditation) to periods of withdrawal, fasting and prayer practiced in some religions, through the various yogic exercises and positions, and perhaps to the whirling of dervishes or the repetitive chants of certain religious rites.* Despite these apparent differences in specifics of the meditative techniques, all have the goal of developeing receptivity for spontaneous, internally generated (physiological or ideational) stimuli. This is some-times referred to as gaining enlightenment.

Interpretations of the meanings or significance of the internally generated stimuli clearly depend on the frame of reference or philosophy underlying the particular practice. Thus, among religious groups meditation (or contemplation, as this term is more commonly used among the religions) is a technique to attain a better realization of God. In contrast, the principle long-range goal of Transcendental Meditation is to develop the full mental potential of the individual, and a feeling of unity with the universe. Regardless of the verbal descriptors used to describe the result, it appears that all meditators are attempting to attain greater sensitivity to subjective states in their many dimensions, and to bring a variety of experiences -- normally assumed to be beyond conscious control or awareness -- into direct awareness.

Although this book is a review of research and other publications about primarily Transcendental Meditation, the materials presented may be applic-able to many or all meditation techniques. Hopefully, the material presented herin will encourage scientists interested in the communalities between all of the various approaches to enlightenment to investigate the similarities in practice and effects of the different techniques.

---

*For a fuller exposition of meditative and contemplative techniques, see References III 1, 4; IV 8, 10; VI 1, 2, 3, 4, 5, 9, 15 in Appendix A.

II PHYSIOLOGICAL CORRELATES

The physiological correlates of TM--and of some of the meditational states reached by other techniques--appear to define a lowered metabolic state characterized by decreased autonomic activity, decreased emotional and sensory reactivity, decreased muscle tension, and a wakeful, alert brain (Orme-Johnson, 1971; Wallace et al., 1971). Changes in the electrical activity of the brain, in the autonomic nervous system, and in somatosensory functions during wakefulness, sleep, and meditation are discussed below.

A.   Electroencephalography

1.   During Wakefulness and Sleep

For each of the major states of wakefulness and the various stages of sleep, there is corresponding electrical activity in the brain, indicated by the electroencephalogram (EEG) or "brain waves." Figure 1 shows portions of a representative EEG recording illustrating changes that occur in brain wave patterns as one progresses from the state of wakefulness to the various stages of sleep and dreaming.

When a person is awake and active, the EEG is characterized by low-amplitude (20 to 40 μV), mixed-frequency brain waves, usually predominated by beta waves (12 to 35 Hz). When the eyes are closed while resting or before going to sleep, trains of alpha waves appear (Figure 1a). These are bursts of brain waves of about 30 to 50 μV peak-to-peak amplitude in the 8- to 12-Hz range. The alpha waves are usually associated with a steady state of relaxed, wakeful alertness (Tart, 1969, p. 485). An external stimulus (such as a noise or a bright light) or an internal stimulus (such as a thought or the twitch of a muscle) may disrupt the alpha wave train and be replaced by beta activity. This latter pattern of activity is usually called alpha-blocking. During the transition from wakefulness to Stage 1 sleep, the alpha waves appear to be replaced by low-voltage (10 to 30 μV) theta waves (roughly 5 to 8 Hz) and some mixed-frequency activity. Stage 1 sleep is also characterized by occasional sharp vertex waves. As time goes by, the person slips into Stage 2 sleep, characterized by short bursts of 14-Hz activity (sleep spindles) and K-complexes (see Figure 1b and c). As the person enters Stages 3 and 4 of sleep ("deep" sleep), the predominant features are large-amplitude (75 to 300 μV peak-to-peak), low-frequency (3 Hz or less) delta waves. The sharp vertex waves and the K-complexes completely disappear (Figure 1d and e).

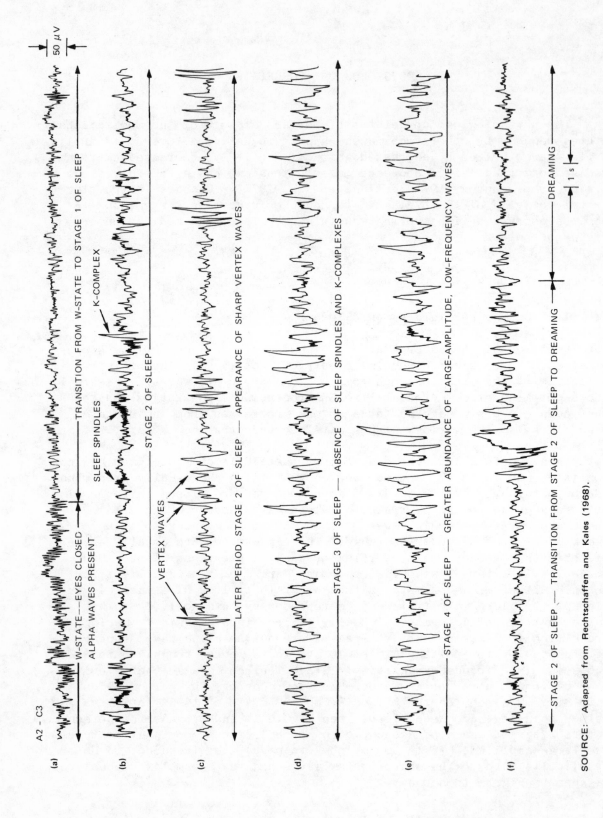

SOURCE: Adapted from Rechtschaffen and Kales (1968).

FIGURE 1 REPRESENTATIVE EEG RECORDS FOR WAKEFULNESS, SLEEP, AND DREAMING

4

After about 90 minutes[*] of sleep as described above, a person may return to either Stage 2 or Stage 1, from which the transition to the dreaming state takes place (Figure 1f). The dreaming state is characterized by low-amplitude (25 to 50 μV peak-to-peak), variable-frequency waves usually accompanied by episodic rapid eye movements (REM) and a quiescent submaxillary electromyogram. Alpha waves of somewhat lower frequency than those found during wakefulness may be present. In general, with the exception of occasional alpha waves, the EEG during dreaming is similar to that of Sleep Stage 1.

2.   During Meditation

The brain waves recorded from well-practiced meditators during the practice of TM are characterized by a "marked" increase of alpha wave trains in the central and frontal regions of the brain (Wallace, 1970b; Wallace et al., 1971; Brown et al., 1972). The amplitude may increase and the frequency of these waves may decrease slightly later on in meditation, until bursts of theta waves appear. Figure 2, from Wallace (1970b), gives an example of EEG recordings from one subject practicing TM. Whether this is a typical record is not known. Wallace called attention to the predominance of alpha waves as the subject begins to meditate (Sample A). The appearance of theta waves in the frontal region (FP1) of the brain is depicted in Sample B, taken during the middle of meditation. Figure 3(a) shows the "marked" increase in the alpha wave energy in the 1-Hz band centered around 9 Hz; for the same subject during the same session, Figure 3(b) shows the energy in a 1-Hz band centered around 7 Hz. The energy associated with the subject's alpha waves from the frontal region (Figure 3a) increased appreciably during meditation.

Wallace (1970a) reported that no habituation of alpha blocking to sound and light stimuli took place during TM. In 25 subjects before, during, and after the practice of TM, Wallace found that the most striking characteristic change in the EEG pattern during TM was an increase in the intensity of the 8- to 9-Hz band (slow alpha waves) in the central and frontal regions. (This does not necessarily indicate, however, that total alpha was increasing.) In some subjects, this increase was accompanied by occasional bursts of 5- to 8-Hz (or theta) waves in the frontal channel. Three subjects who reported that they were tired before meditation experienced some drowsiness as they began meditation. Drowsiness and slight sleep frequently accompany the practice of TM, especially in novice meditators. Their drowsiness was confirmed in the EEG records by prominent activity in the theta range, characteristic of Sleep Stage 1 (Rechtschaffen and Kales, 1968). As their meditation continued, the Sleep Stage 1 pattern was replaced by more regular alpha activity. Wallace reported (1970b, p. 18) that, according to the subjects, "... meditation is such that if a person is

_____

[*]This time varies with age, usually being 40-45 minutes for infants and about two hours for the aged (Hartman, 1967).

SUBJECT 19

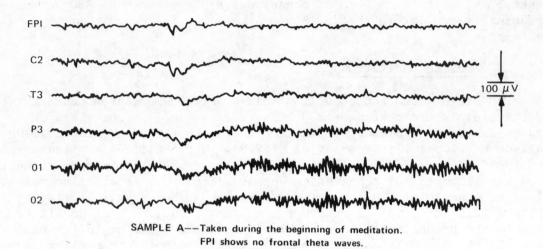

FPI
C2
T3
P3
01
02

100 μV

SAMPLE A——Taken during the beginning of meditation.
FPI shows no frontal theta waves.

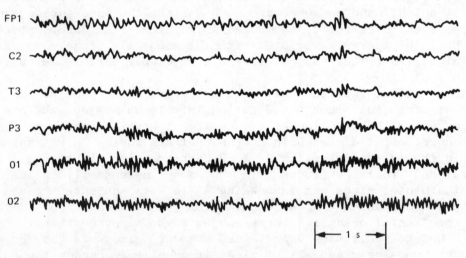

FP1
C2
T3
P3
01
02

|← 1 s →|

SAMPLE B——Taken during the middle of meditation.
Shows pronounced theta trains in the
frontal lead (FPI).

SOURCE: Adapted from Wallace (1970b).

FIGURE 2   EEG RECORDINGS TAKEN FROM THE SAME SUBJECT
DURING TM

6

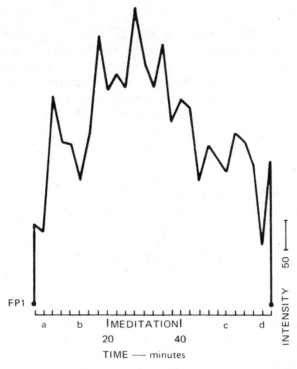

SUBJECT 5

FP1

INTENSITY

50

a   b |MEDITATION| c   d

20   40

TIME — minutes

(a) FREQUENCY = 9.0 Hz

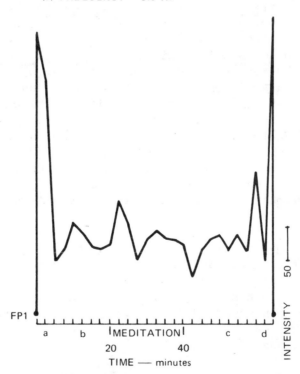

SUBJECT 5

FP1

INTENSITY

50

a   b |MEDITATION| c   d

20   40

TIME — minutes

(b) FREQUENCY = 7.0 Hz

SOURCE: Adapted from Wallace (1970b).

FIGURE 3   POWER SPECTRAL DENSITY CURVES IN 1-Hz BANDWIDTHS FOR ONE
SUBJECT, SHOWING THE INCREASE IN INTENSITY OF ALPHA WAVES
DURING PRACTICE OF TM

The subject was sitting with his eyes closed between a and b, practicing TM
between b and c, and sitting with his eyes closed between c and d.   The
alpha frequency of this subject was between 9 and 10 Hz.

7

overly tired before meditation, the easiness and relaxation of the
process will naturally allow him to fall into a short sleep which is
later replaced by the clear experience of meditation." It should be
noted here that the appearance of alpha and theta waves in both the
transcendental state and the early sleep stages makes the distinction
between the two states by the use of the EEG alone somewhat equivocal,
given the present state of our knowledge. The significance, if any,
of the apparent similarities between the TC-state and Sleep Stage 1
remains to be determined.

Onda (1965), Akishige (1968), and Kasamatsu and Hirai (1966) indicate that as soon as Zen meditators begin to progress from wakefulness
to the meditation state, alpha activity of 10-12 Hz begins to appear.
Later on, the amplitude of the alpha waves increases, and subsequently
their frequency decreases to 7-8 Hz. For those who have "mastered" the
Zen technique of meditation, the frequency of the brain waves decreases
further until "pure" theta waves (5-6 Hz) predominate.

In a companion study to the main SRI study, Vassiliadis (1973)
obtained EEG data from the frontal and occipital regions of novice TM
and control subjects. After transducers were placed on the subject,
physiological data were collected over a period of one hour. The
subject initially sat quietly with eyes open (10 minutes) followed by
a 10-minute period with eyes closed. Subsequently, he either meditated
or rested (control condition) for 20 minutes. Finally, there was a
second period of sitting quietly with eyes closed (10 minutes) followed
by a final 10-minute period with eyes open. (See also Otis, Kanellakos,
Lukas, and Vassiliades, p. 84, Ref. 31 in Appendix A, Section I.B. for
procedural details.) The recorded data were analyzed by passing the
EEG signals through band-pass filters of 8-12 Hz for alpha wave content
and of 5-7 Hz for theta wave content. The outputs of the filters were
passed through root-mean-square reading meters, integrated, and recorded.
This gave a continuous indication of the signal power in the alpha and
theta (5-7 Hz) wave bands of the spectrum of the EEG signals; it did not,
however, give any indication of brain wave frequency changes within the
filter bandwidths.

A preliminary examination of the EEG data was made, comparing
subjects after three to four months of meditation or control procedures.
Also, a preliminary analysis was made in which the EEG records of
meditators before starting TM were compared with their own records after
six to nine months of meditation. The comparisons were made in terms
of normalized data so that each individual receives equal weight in the
statistical analysis.

Before beginning the practice of meditation, both meditator and
control groups showed similar characteristics in the frontal region.
In contrast with Wallace's data (Wallace, 1970b), there were no

8

statistically significant changes in the frontal region over the six to nine months of meditation.[*]

In the occipital region, however, although meditators and controls showed similar characteristics before the practice was begun, significant changes were seen in both alpha and theta content as a function of length of practice of TM.

During the period just prior to meditation, the alpha power in the occipital region showed a characteristic decrease from the initial closing of the eyes until the second eyes-closed period, at which time there was an increase in power. After three to four months of meditation, the meditators showed somewhat higher alpha than the controls in the second half of meditation and in both of the eyes-open conditions. At the end of six to nine months of meditation (as compared with the same group before meditation), although there was no statistically significant difference during the meditation period, there was a significant increase in the alpha power during the second eyes-closed period over that during the first eyes-closed period. In addition, it was noted that the alpha content during both eyes-open periods was also higher.

The theta wave content in the occipital region also showed some changes. Before the beginning of practice of meditation, the theta power in general decreased somewhat throughout the recording session, and the theta content was lower at the end than at the beginning of the recording period. After six to nine months of meditation, there was a significant gradual increase in theta wave power during meditation, and the theta content was higher at the end than at the beginning of the recording session.

Theta waves have been seen after about 25 minutes of continuous meditation in Zen masters who have practiced Zen meditation for more than 20 years (Akishige, 1968; Kasamatsu and Hirai, 1966). Kasamatsu and Hirai reported that Zen masters go through four stages during Zen meditation; appearance of alpha activity with the beginning of meditation (Stage 1), increase in the amplitude of the alpha waves (Stage 2), decrease in the frequency of the alpha waves (Stage 3), and appearance of theta waves (Stage 4). It should be noted that the theta waves could be interpreted as being associated with drowsiness or sleep since it is known that theta activity is prominent during Sleep Stage 1.

---

[*]It should be noted, however, that Wallace's subjects were well-seasoned meditators (average of 32 months of meditation), whereas Vassiliadis' subjects had practiced meditation for only 3-9 months. The differences noted may be related to length of time of practice of TM or, possibly, to inevitable subject selection that occurs when data are reported for subjects who are sufficiently motivated to continue the practice of TM for almost 3 years.

Onda (1965) and Kasamatsu and Hirai (1966) observed in Zen practitioners that the alpha waves were blocked for about 3 to 4 seconds, apparently without habituation, whereas the theta waves were also suppressed or blocked by "click" stimuli, but the blocking of theta waves did habituate.

A "marked" increase in alpha activity was reported to have occurred in four subjects practicing Raja Yoga (Anand et al., 1961). Two of the yogis were exposed to external stimuli (visual, auditory, thermal, and vibratory). None of these stimuli produced any blocking of the alpha waves when the yogis were meditating, but all the stimuli blocked the alpha waves if the yogis were not meditating but resting with eyes closed. All yogis showed prominent alpha activity during their resting periods as well. One of the yogis while meditating was oblivious to the cold and pain presumably caused by having his hand immersed in a bucket of ice water kept at 4°C. Apparently there was no change in the EEG with the immersion.

Attempts have been made in the laboratory to "teach" subjects to "control" their alpha wave activity, that is, to learn to turn their alpha waves on and off or to extend the alpha duration at will (Kamiya, 1968, 1969; Stoyva and Kamiya, 1968; Tart, 1969, p. 485). It has been found that meditators, as compared with nonmeditators, learn to control their alpha waves relatively quickly during biofeedback training (Kamiya, 1969). In general, the reports of these subjects about their feelings while they were generating alpha waves (Luce, 1965; Kamiya, 1968, 1969; Stoyva and Kamiya, 1968) were similar to those of subjects who used "natural" meditation (Deikman, 1963, 1966a,b) or other forms of meditation (Maupin, 1962, 1965; Kondo, 1952, 1958; Maharishi Mahesh Yogi, 1966). In passing, it may be noted that the subjective reports of feeling states during alpha generation of biofeedback or during Zen and TM are similar to those reported during Sleep Stage 1. It should be evident that much more work is needed to understand the relationship of EEG brain waves to the various states of arousal and relaxation.

B.   Electrooculograms (EOG)

Electrooculograms (EOG) are a measure of eye movements. During sleep, eye movements are either very slow or are not observed at all. However, periodically throughout the night, episodic rapid eye movements (REM) occur. These, together with activity of certain head muscles (i.e., those of the lower chin) and the pattern of brain activity, define whether or not a person is dreaming (Rechtschaffen and Kales, 1968). Wallace (1970b) reported no apparent REM during the practice of TM in five subjects, although other types of eye movements did occur. This finding indicates that, at least in one respect, the TC-state is different from the REM stage of sleep.

10

C.   Electromyograms (EMG) and Body Motility

Das and Gastaut (1955) reported that in meditating yogis, no peripheral muscular activity could be detected although the yogis were
sitting with erect bodies, but in relaxed positions. The sensitivity
of the measuring instruments, however, may not have permitted recording
of low-amplitude EMG activity. Similarly, during the yogi breathing
exercise, "shavasan," EMG potentials dropped to almost zero (Datey et
al., 1969).

Japanese scientists (reported in Akishige, 1968) have studied the
EMG of persons practicing various forms of Zen meditation. They found
that the muscular tone of Zen monks was one-half that of laymen (control
subjects) and that the duration of muscle contractions increased as the
elapsed time into meditation increased. In the case of contraction of
the muscle extensor communis (a long, narrow muscle on the dorsal forearm that straightens the fingers), the duration was 1.83 seconds at 5
minutes after the beginning of meditation, 2.23 seconds at 20 minutes
into meditation, and as long as 2.80 seconds when 40 minutes of meditation had elapsed.

A person practicing TM usually assumes a relaxed, quiet, sitting
pose; yet formications, tics, and localized muscle spasms may appear.
Electromyographic studies of individuals in TM have been undertaken at
Stanford Research Institute (Otis, Kanellakos, Lukas and Vassiliadis,
1972). The EMGs generally were high during the initial eyes-open period (10 minutes) and then gradually reduced in amplitude as the experimental recording period entered the eyes-closed (10 minutes) and rest/
meditation (20 minutes) periods. Near the end of the test session
(second 10-minute period of eyes-closed and second 10 minutes of eyes-
open), the EMG amplitude increased or decreased.

In general, the TM subjects in the SRI experiment exhibited more ($p <$
.05) reduction of potential in the trapezius (neck and shoulder) muscle
after three months of practicing meditation than did the control groups
during comparable periods of resting with the eyes closed.

D.   Respiration Rate

Marked decreases in the respiration rates of Zen meditators have
been observed by Hirai and Sugi (cited in Kasamatsu and Hirai, 1966, and
Akishige, 1968). Onda (1965) reported that in certain Zen practitioners,
respiration slowed to 2 or 3 breaths per minute from a rate of about 15
breaths per minute while they were awake and not meditating.

Bagchi and Wenger (1957) reported decreases in respiration rate of
up to 50 or 60 percent (average of 23 percent) in yogis during meditation. In hypertensive patients performing "shavasan" (a yogi exercise),
Datey et al. (1969) found breath rates of 8 per minute compared to 22
per minute during nonexercise periods.

Allison (1970) noted a reduction in breath rate from about 12 per minute to an average of about 6 per minute during the meditation period of a person practicing TM (see Figure 4). Five persons practicing TM were reported by Wallace (1970a) to obtain an average decrease of about 3 breaths per minute (from 13.5 to 10.5). Wallace and Benson (1972) reported that the volume per breath also decreased during TM.

Vassiliadis (1973) measured respiration rate by placing a thermistor at the end of the nose within $\frac{1}{2}$ inch of the nostrils of both novice TM and control subjects. Measurements were not taken prior to the start of meditation, so that before and after comparisons cannot be made. After four months of meditation, the respiratory rate of the meditator group was about 20 percent less than that of the control group (significant at the 0.02 level of confidence).

Respiration rates decrease rapidly prior to sleep. For example, Hauri (1968) found an average decrease of about 1 breath per minute in 15 subjects after they had been in bed roughly 5 minutes. Decreases of about 23 percent (5 breaths per minute) were reported by Malmo (1959) in three subjects. Although his results probably are applicable to the changes between Sleep Stage 1 and Stages 3 and 4 (within the first hour of sleep) and consequently are not directly applicable to the earliest period of sleep, they are included here to indicate how quickly and the extent to which respiration rates change during sleep. During dreaming, the breathing rate fluctuates and may reach values of vigorous exercise (Snyder, 1963, 1967, 1971; Luce, 1965, 1970).

E.   Heart Rate

Reported changes of heart rate while in yoga meditation have been contradictory. For example, Das and Gastaut (1955) reported an increase from about 70 to 78 beats per minute in yogis practicing yoga postures and meditation; after meditation it dropped to about 60. On the other hand, Bagchi and Wenger (1957) reported that no consistent changes took place during yoga meditation.

With TM, in contrast, decreases in heart rate are usually reported. Wallace (1970a,b) reported that the mean heart rate of 11 subjects practicing TM decreased significantly, with a mean decrease of about 5 beats per minute.

Vassiliadis (1972) found that the changes in heart rate of novice meditators and controls were not significantly different at the end of three to four months of meditation; the decrease in heart rate during meditation from that during a rest period just prior to meditation was comparable to the decrease observed in the controls during their "rest" period. It was also observed, however, that there was a significant increase (p < .02) in the resting or initial heart rate of the meditators after four months of meditation compared with their rate before learning

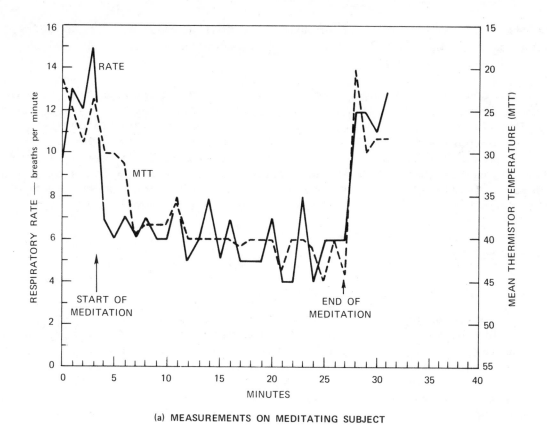

(a) MEASUREMENTS ON MEDITATING SUBJECT

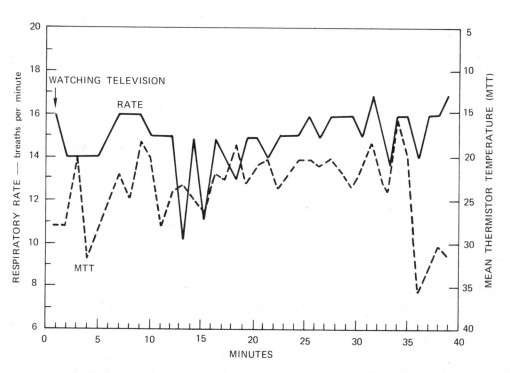

(b) CONTROL MEASUREMENTS WHILE SUBJECT WAS WATCHING TELEVISION

SOURCE: Adapted from Allison (1970).

FIGURE 4   CHANGES IN MTT AND RESPIRATORY RATE DURING TM

meditation. After six to nine months of meditation, heart rate decreased significantly during meditation as compared with controls (5% and 2%, respectively; p < .05).

In contrast, the mean decrease in heart rate per minute during sleep varies from about 2 to 12 beats, depending on such factors as age and sex. Fluctuations are observed in the heart rate during dreaming periods, sometimes increasing to values of vigorous activity (Kleitman, 1963; Luce, 1965; Hartman, 1967; Snyder, 1967). On the average, however, the heart rate decreases about 12 beats per minute after about 4.5 hours of sleep (Snyder, 1971). Hauri (1968) found reductions of about 2 beats per minute about 5 minutes after the subjects had gone to bed.

F. Blood Pressure

1. During Meditation

Systolic blood pressure has been reported to rise minimally in a few cases (Bagchi and Wenger, 1957). In two instances, it dropped 20 "points" (percentage points, presumably) at the end of the meditation period. In another case, Hatha Yoga meditators showed no change; one measurement was taken before and one after meditation, the latter being preceded by yoga postures. Wallace et al. (1971) and Wallace and Benson (1972) have reported that the blood pressure does not change significantly during TM.

2. Longitudinal Studies

Datey et al. (1969) reported that over a period of 30 to 40 weeks, an average decrease of about 20 percent in systolic blood pressure was observed in 47 hypertensive patients who were practicing "shavasan" breathing exercises (this decrease was observed outside the period of practicing shavasan).

It has been reported, anecdotally, that in several persons who have taken up the practice of TM, "dangerously" high blood pressures have been lowered to safe levels, to the point where some of the subjects were taken off medication (Anonymous, 1969). These, of course, might represent spontaneous remissions that are unrelated to the practice of TM. As mentioned above, Wallace et al. (1971) have reported that the blood pressure does not change appreciably during TM.

Changes in blood pressure of meditators may be difficult to evaluate since most meditators are young--and those who take up meditation may have unusually low pressure to begin with. For example, Schmit (1971) reported an average blood pressure of about 109/65 in a group of 20 practitioners of TM. The mean age of this group of males and females was 26 years and they had been meditating for about 29 months. The spread in duration of practice was remarkable--between one month and five years. However, there appeared to be little correlation between duration of practice and either systolic or diastolic blood pressure.

14

Included in a questionnaire dealing with subjective behavioral and physiological effects of TM (Otis, private communication, 1971) that was sent to 1900 randomly selected practitioners was a question about possible changes in blood pressure. Only 12 subjects (8 males and 4 females), out of the 525 who responded, indicated that high blood pressure was a "problem" for them before taking up TM. Of these, three reported no change and nine indicated changes (six, a moderate decrease; two, a considerable decrease; and one, a complete normalization). In addition, two subjects reported abnormally low blood pressure prior to taking up TM, and both indicated a moderate increase after starting TM. The frequency of such changes is so low, however, that chance factors may explain their occurrence.

Otis, Jones and Sjoberg (1972) studied changes in blood pressure of 31 volunteers who applied to SIMS (Stanford University Chapter) for training in TM. Measures were taken before TM training and monthly thereafter for six months. The means and standard deviations for diastolic blood pressure before and at the end of six months of meditation were 120.1 ± 16.1 and 119.8 ± 15.4 mm Hg, respectively. There were no significant changes in either systolic or diastolic pressure noted for this group, seven of whom had systolic blood pressures exceeding 130 mm Hg during the pretest. Also, increases, decreases or no changes over the six-month period were not correlated with regularity of the practice of TM.

The main SRI experiment (Otis, Kanellakos, Lukas and Vassiliadis, p.84) involved 60 normal subjects whose blood pressure was monitored once a month for three months prior to initiation of meditation or control conditions; the average value of the three monthly readings was 123.6/69.2 mm Hg. Although differences between TM and control groups never materialized, two of the TM subjects who were hypertensive and under medical treatment had lower blood pressure and were gradually taken off medication by their physicians after a few months of TM practice; their blood pressure remained low after 12 months of TM practice. However, the blood pressure of four other subjects with hypertensive patterns was unaffected by the practice of TM.

3.   During Sleep and Dreaming

In contrast, variations that occur during sleep are as follows. Shortly after going to bed and before the onset of sleep, there is an initial drop of about 5 mm Hg in systolic blood pressure (assuming 120 mm Hg as a basal average) followed by a drop in diastolic blood pressure. Another abrupt decrease of about 10 mm Hg is typically observed and is closely correlated with the onset of sleep (Snyder, 1971). Thus, within a half hour after going to bed, systolic blood pressure drops about 15 mm Hg, or roughly 13 percent. Blood pressure also fluctuates during dreaming. These fluctuations may be related to the autonomic nervous system "storms" that occur during this state of consciousness (Snyder, 1967; Luce, 1971). Blood pressure varies over wide limits during wakefulness, depending on activity and emotionality.

G. Skin Resistance

A rise in skin resistance generally indicates increased relaxation and decreased tension. With certain types of yogi meditation, the galvanic skin resistance (measured across the palm of one hand) increases gradually from 70 to 100 percent as the meditation period progresses (Bagchi and Wenger, 1957).

Wallace (1970a,b) and Wallace et al. (1971) reported that within minutes after starting meditation, skin resistance increased by 160 percent on the average, and up to 500 percent in some individual subjects. A dramatic example of these changes in skin resistance for a single subject is shown in Figure 5. Increases in skin resistance of TM practitioners during a stress-inducing task have been reported by Orme-Johnson (1973). (See Section III, A2, pp. 23-28.)

During sleep, skin resistance may rise to a level 130 percent above that of the awake level in the course of several hours of sleep (Kleitman, 1963). Bohlin (1971) indicated that skin resistance increased about 13 percent, on the average, in the first 2-3 minutes of a test session conducive to resting and sleep, but that 13 minutes were required before the resistance increased 22 percent over basal levels. These findings suggest that the results described by Wallace may be attributed, at least in part, to a rapidly induced general relaxation--approximating sleep--on the part of the subjects, and not solely to a process unique to TM.

H. Energy Metabolism

Onda (1965) reported a decrease of the metabolic rate in Zen meditators of up to 35 percent, and Sugi et al. (cited in Kasamatsu and Hirai, 1969) reported a decrease of energy metabolism in Zen meditators, but did not cite any figures. Akishige (1968), who summarized many studies of individual Zen masters, reported an average metabolic rate decrease of about 15 percent, ranging between 5 and 25 percent.

Basal metabolic rates have not been measured directly during sleep, but it has been reported (Snyder, 1971) that during the first seven hours of a night's sleep, oxygen consumption decreased about 10 percent, on the average, relative to pre-sleep values. These results indicate some reduction in metabolic rate during sleep.

I. Skin and Body Temperatures

Skin temperature during the practice of yogi meditation was measured by Bagchi and Wenger (1957). A drop of $1^{O}C$ was noted 10 minutes after the beginning of meditation. Wallace et al (1971) reported that rectal temperature did not change during TM. Measurements of five subjects were

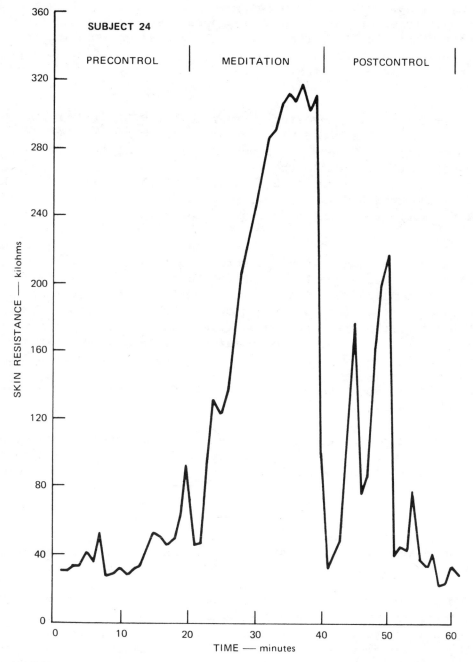

SOURCE: Adapted from Wallace (1970b).

FIGURE 5   CHANGE IN SKIN RESISTANCE OF ONE SUBJECT
PRACTICING TM

17

made before, during, and after meditation; the average temperature was $37.4 \pm 0.3^{\circ}C$ during meditation, $0.1^{\circ}C$ higher before, and $0.1^{\circ}C$ lower after meditation.

An unpublished report from Germany (Ritterstaedt, 1966) stated that surface temperatures of the forehead increased between 0.4 and $1.6^{\circ}C$ in all subjects practicing TM. The preliminary report gave no indication of the temperature changes in nonmeditators. An infrared radiometer was used to obtain these measurements. It had an accuracy of $0.03^{\circ}C$ and was insensitive to background radiation.

In a similar preliminary study, Franz Holl (1971) used an AGA Thermovision camera to take infrared pictures of eight well-practiced (several years of practice) meditators. The subject sat quietly for about 60 minutes to become acclimatized to the laboratory temperature. In general, increases in skin temperature of 0.5 to $1.0^{\circ}C$ in the throat and forehead areas and of 0.5 to $3.5^{\circ}C$ in the forearm were evident. Nonmeditators showed skin temperature changes "somewhat" lower than those of the meditators.

Ritterstaedt and Schenkluhn (private communication, 1972) have repeated temperature measurements of the forehead skin (area between the eyebrows) on a small number of well-practiced (i.e., 5 to 10 years) meditators, using a temperature-dependent diode. They have found that invariably when the subjects were rested (i.e., during the morning meditation on working days and during the morning or afternoon meditation on non-working days), the forehead temperature increased by about $0.7-0.8^{\circ}C$. When the subjects were tired, however, the forehead temperature invariably decreased 0.2 to $0.7^{\circ}C$. The significance of these results, if repeatable, however, is not clear.

Vassiliadis (1972) used thermocouples to measure skin temperatures of the forehead and arm of novice transcendental meditators (meditating less than six months) and control subjects. Temperature was monitored by very small thermocouples in contact with the skin, and a reference junction was placed in a water bath in order to maintain a constant reference temperature. In contrast with the results from Germany (Ritterstaedt, above) for advanced meditators, the forehead temperature of novice meditators decreased as the session progressed, with a slight warming at the end. However, the forehead temperature of the meditator group did not decrease as much as that of the control group ($p < .05$, one-tailed test). The temperature of the hand, in contrast, increased during the recording sessions, with some decrease toward the end of the session. The average hand temperature of the meditator group increased more than that of the control group ($p = .07$). These hand temperature changes are consistent with those reported by Holl (1971).

Shortly after going to bed, skin temperature shows an initial increase of about $0.5^{\circ}C$, followed by a gradual decline over several hours to a level about $0.5^{\circ}C$ lower than the basal level. In contrast, rectal temperatures show a gradual decline of about $1^{\circ}C$ during the first five hours of sleep, followed by an increase toward the basal level (Snyder, 1971).

In general, the temperature changes observed during meditation appear to be of the same magnitude found during sleep. However, during meditation the changes may occur more rapidly.

J.   Oxygen Consumption, CO_2 Elimination, Blood Gases and pH

Wallace et al. (1970a) reported that during the TC-state, respiration is reduced in rate and amplitude, oxygen consumption goes down, and the metabolic rate decreases 5 to 10 minutes after the beginning of the meditation period. Total oxygen consumption decreased by an average of 40 cc/min (from normal levels of 110 to 140 $cc/min/m^2$ of body surface area, presumably), and CO_2 output decreased about 30 cc/min (from normal levels of 88-120 $cc/min/m^2$ of body surface area). The respiratory exchange quotient (CO_2/O_2), however, did not change appreciably from the basal range (0.77-0.90). Figure 6 shows the time course of changes in O_2 consumption.

Arterial pCO_2, pO_2, and pH of ten subjects were measured during TM by Wallace and co-workers (1970b, 1971). In most of the 10 subjects practicing TM, they found a slight decrease in arterial pH ($p < .05$); the mean decrease was 0.01 pH units. Arterial pO_2 and pCO_2 did not fluctuate significantly during practice of meditation. However, using a nomogram and the obtained pH and pCO_2 levels to calculate base excess, a significant ($p < .005$) decrease of 1.0 meq/liter was found. They concluded that TM results in a "mild" condition of metabolic acidosis.

The pH of blood in Zen monks was reported to drop slightly (0.03 to 0.04 pH units) during Zen meditation (Akishige, 1968). Uropepsin output decreased significantly in a group of students after three weeks of performing yoga postures daily for 1.5 hours (Karambelkar et al., 1969). The postures presumably relax the body and the mind and, in turn, the mind affects the functioning of the internal organs and glands.

During one study, the concentration of CO_2 in the blood during sleep increased by 4.4% and the pH of blood changed from 7.52 to 7.40, whereas the pH of saliva changed from 6.7 to 6.3 (Kleitman, 1963). It is clear, on the basis of the available data, that the pH of the blood changes more after several hours of sleep (about 0.10 units) than it does after 20 to 30 minutes of either TM or Zen meditation (about 0.01 to 0.04 units, respectively).

K.   Cardiac Output

Changes in cardiac blood flow are a measure of metabolic rate; the flow rate is proportional to the amount of oxygen carried to the tissues

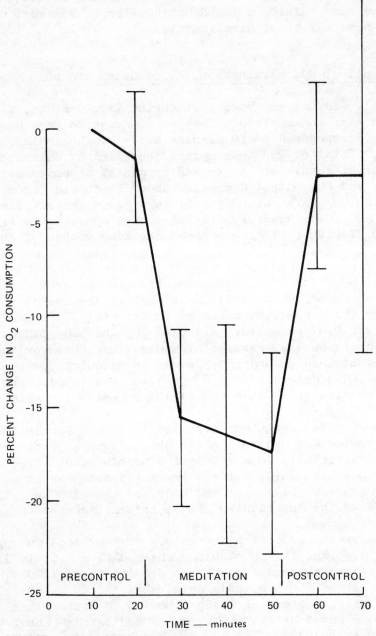

SOURCE: Adapted from Wallace (1970b).

FIGURE 6   MEAN PERCENTAGE CHANGE IN TOTAL OXYGEN
CONSUMPTION FOR FIFTEEN SUBJECTS BEFORE,
DURING, AND AFTER PRACTICE OF TM

20

and used in metabolic processes. Wallace (1970b), by means of catheters inserted in the veins of five subjects before a test session, observed a significant (p < .005) mean decrease of about 25 percent in the cardiac output during TM.

The decreases in total oxygen consumption and cardiac output (as measured by heart rate) during TM and sleep appear to be of the same order of magnitude, indicating that a lower metabolic rate and rest characterize the system. During TM, however, the decreases take place within a few minutes, whereas in sleep the drop usually requires considerably more time.

L. Lactate Ion Concentration in Blood

Lactate concentration in blood has been found to decrease during TM. Wallace et al. (1971) found that the average blood lactate level in eight subjects decreased significantly (p < .005) during TM (from 11.4 ± 4.1 mg/100 ml in the premeditation period to 8.0 ± 2.6 mg/100 ml). Also, it stayed low in the period following meditation (7.3 ± 2.0 mg/100 ml). The rate of decrease during the first 10 minutes of TM was about 300 percent greater than during simple rest with eyes closed. [See also Pitts (1969) and p. 118, this book.]

A summary of the major physiological correlates of the wakeful, deep sleep, dreaming, and transcendental states is presented in Table 1.[*]

-----

[*] Since Table 1 was prepared in 1972, several papers have appeared that have not been included in column headed "Transcendental State." [Editor]

Table 1

A SUMMARY OF THE MAJOR PHYSIOLOGICAL CORRELATES
OF FOUR STATES OF HUMAN CONSCIOUSNESS

PHYSIOLOGIC PARAMETER	WAKEFULNESS	DEEP SLEEP (Stages 3 and 4)	DREAMING	TRANSCENDENTAL STATE
EEG	Low amplitude (20-40 μv), predominantly beta waves (17-35 Hz).	High amplitude (above 75 μv) delta waves (0.5-3 Hz) predominate.	Low amplitude (12-25 μv), variable frequencies resembling Sleep Stage 1; occasional "sawtooth" waves.	Alpha waves (8-12 Hz) in central and frontal regions. Bursts of theta waves (4-7 Hz) may be found in frontal region. Experienced meditators are reported to show, in general, "more prominent" alpha than nonmeditators. Increase in occipital alpha and theta power in novice meditators.
RESPIRATION RATE	Variable, depending on activity, ranging between 10 and 25 breaths per minute.	Reported to decrease about 23% (or 5 breaths per minute) by the time the subject attains the first period of deep sleep (about 1 hour from onset of sleep).	Variable, probably depending on dream content. At times may attain levels found in vigorous activity.	Variable rates are reported, but decreases are typical. Rates as low as 2-3 breaths per minute are reported in some Zen practitioners. For transcendental meditators, rates of 4-15 breaths have been reported during mediation.
HEART RATE	Varies with activity. Average of 70 beats per minute is common in the seated subject.	Variable slowing of from 2 to 12 beats, depending on age and sex. Decreases of about 12 beats per minute found after 4½ hours of sleep.	Fluctuations noted during dreams. Rate apparently may vary with dream content. At times may attain levels found during vigorous activity.	Results are somewhat contradictory. In yogis, increases or no changes in rate were reported. During TM, in contrast, average decreases of 3 to 5 beats were reported. Slight increases have also been found, however,
BLOOD PRESSURE	Average pressure varies somewhat — about 120 (systolic) and 80 (diastolic). May vary as a function of activity.	A progressive drop accompanies resting prior to sleep. Decrease is about 15 mm Hg (systolic) ½ hour after going to bed (presumably during Stage 2). During Stages 3 and 4, may decrease another 2-3 mm Hg.	Higher, on the average, during REM stage than during Sleep Stages 3 and 4 and shows greater variability.	As with heart rate, ambiguous results reported for yogis. Studies of TM suggest no change during mediation.
SKIN RESISTANCE	Variable, depending on activity. Typically decreases when subject is under stress, increases when subject is relaxed.	In the course of several hours of sleep, increases an average of 130%, but it increased about 13% in the first 2-3 minutes in a situation conducive to sleep. In 13 minutes, increased 22% over basal levels.	Some variability, apparently related to dream content. On the average, levels are near those found during Sleep Stages 3 and 4.	Increased to twice basal levels with some forms of yoga meditation. During TM, increased an average of 160% within minutes.
OXYGEN CONSUMPTION	Changes according to ongoing activity. During vigorous exercise, can attain twice normal resting levels.	Decreases of 10-20% have been found during Stages 3 and 4, while CO$_2$ concentration increases 4-6.25%.	Higher during REM stage than during Stages 3 and 4. May be related to the activity content of dreams.	Average decreases of about 17% found during TM. In certain Zen meditators, decreases of 20-30% have been reported. No changes in CO$_2$ concentration.
LACTIC ACID	Increases with stress, activity; generally, acid level is correlated with level of fatigue. Levels generally decrease with rest and relaxation.	Acid levels decrease during Stages 3 and 4; amount of decrease has not been specified clearly.	Little or no data.	Decreases of 33% have been found. During the first 10 minutes of TM, blood lactate levels have been reported to decrease 3 times faster than when just sitting.

22

III   PSYCHOLOGICAL CORRELATES

Several studies on the psychological correlates of individuals who voluntarily take up TM, or on changes in personality or behavior of practitioners as a function of the length of time they have been practicing TM, have appeared in the literature. Those studies known to us during the first edition of the SRI report appear below. Others can be found in Appendix A (pp. 57 to 120).

A.   Experimental Psychological Studies

1.   Reaction Times

Figure 7 shows average simple reaction times (including movement time) of nine transcendental meditators and nine nonmeditators studied by Shaw and Kolb (1971) at the University of Texas. Each trial consisted of responding to a light flash by moving the hand from a resting position to press a buttom 20 cm away. Each point in the figure is an average of 90 trials (10 for each subject). The average reaction times for meditators before meditation were faster than those of nonmeditators before rest. In a second test, the average reaction times of meditators after 20 minutes of meditation were faster than in the first test, but those of nonmeditators after 20 minutes of resting with the eyes closed were slower than in the first test. The statistical significance of these data was not provided by the authors. Nonparametric statistics (the Sign Test), however, which take into account only the relative direction of the corresponding means of the meditators versus the nonmeditators, showed statistically significant differences ($p < .004$ for a two-tailed test) between the distributions of means for both tests.

Similar results have been reported by Brown et al. (1972). They suggest that performance of perceptual tasks, like simple and complex reaction time tasks, by short-term meditators (weeks to a few months of meditation) possibly improved after 20 minutes of TM practice, but that the performance of control subjects worsened after 20 minutes of ordinary rest with the eyes closed. In a pilot study, Blasdell (1971) found that 15 meditators performed significantly "better" on a perceptual motor task (the Mirror Star-Tracing Task) than a similar group of nonmeditators ($p < .05$).

2.   Habituation of GSR

The resistance of the skin to a slight electric current is fairly constant when a person is resting or experiencing minimum stress. Shortly after the appearance of some stressful internal or external

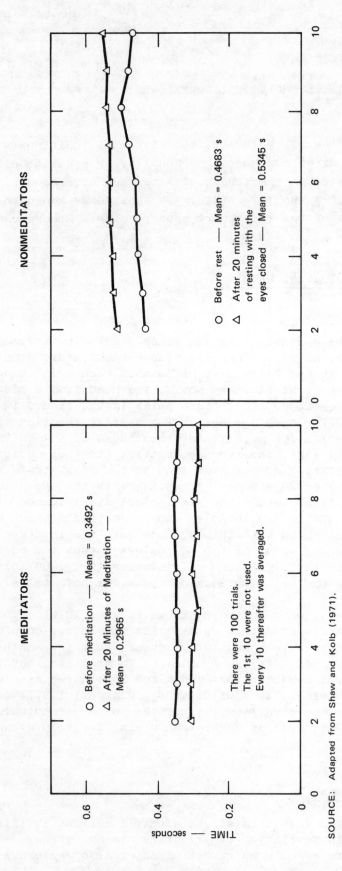

SOURCE: Adapted from Shaw and Kolb (1971).

FIGURE 7   COMPOSITE OF REACTION AND MOVEMENT TIME OF NINE MEDITATORS AND NINE NONMEDITATORS (mean of 90 trials per data point) stimulus, the skin resistance drops. The delay in onset of the resistance change after the onset of the stimulus is called latency. Within limits, the amplitude of the GSR decrease is typically directly related to the amount of stress experienced. As the stress is repeated, the magnitude of the response decreases. A gradual reduction in amplitude of the GSR or its cessation is called "habituation." Habituation presumably protects the system from being overloaded by inputs that are not significant to the organism. The more quickly one is able to habituate, the less stress, of a given type, will he be subjected to.

Illustrated in Figure 8 are the habituation curves for eight meditators and eight nonmeditators in response to tone pulses of 100 dB (with respect to 0.0002 microbar, presumably) at 3000 Hz, with a duration of 0.5 seconds (Orme-Johnson, 1971). Although the two groups of subjects had nearly identical response magnitudes to the initial tone pulses, the meditators showed almost no response after about 15 trials, whereas the nonmeditators continued to show a slight response even after 40 presentations of the tone pulse. These results show that the meditators were able to habituate to the noise pulses more rapidly than the nonmeditators.

Galvanic skin responses are observed in response to external stimuli (such as bursts of noise) as well as to no obvious external stimuli. The latter phenomena are called spontaneous GSRs. The functional significance of spontaneous GSRs is poorly understood, but for the purposes of this presentation they may be considered to be physiological events generated by internal stimuli, modulated by the autonomic nervous system. The "average" person in the laboratory shows about 35 spontaneous GSRs (with amplitudes proportional to decreases in GSR of about 100 ohms or greater) every 10 minutes. Illustrated in Figure 9 is the number of spontaneous GSRs of a group of nonmeditators sitting quietly with eyes open and closed and under threat of electrical shock (Katkin, after Orme-Johnson, 1973*). A similar study, which did not use the threat of electrical shock, was conducted by Orme-Johnson (1971) with groups of meditators and nonmeditators; these results are also shown in Figure 9. In general, the meditators showed fewer spontaneous GSRs than did the nonmeditators (about 9 per 10 minutes for meditators versus 35 per 10 minutes for nonmeditators) during Session 1. The decrease between Sessions 1 and 2 (roughly 10 every 10 minutes) in the number of spontaneous GSRs observed in the nonmeditator group suggests that the frequency of spontaneous GSRs may be related, in part, to the subject's increased familiarity with the laboratory environment.

Orme-Johnson indicated that the subjects had been studied once in Session 1 and twice in Session 2. Nevertheless, if it is assumed that both groups were equally familiar with the laboratory environment, the

---

*Recent personal communication.

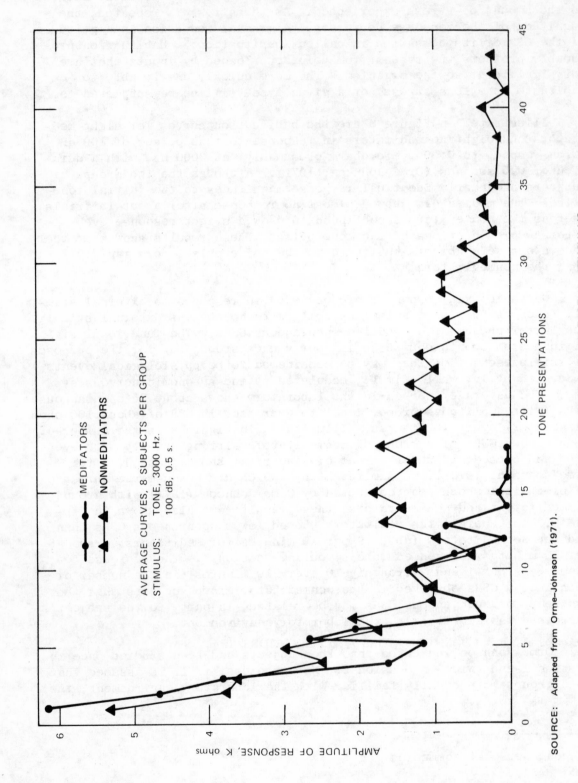

FIGURE 8   HABITUATION TO A STRESSFUL STIMULUS

SOURCE: Adapted from Orme–Johnson (1971).

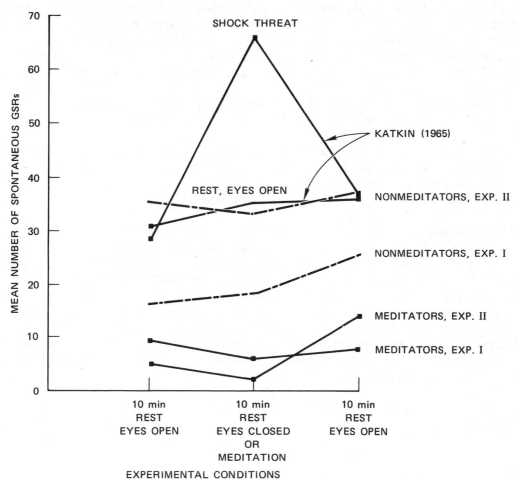

SOURCE: Adapted from Orme–Johnson (1971) and Katkin (1965).

FIGURE 9   MEAN NUMBER OF SPONTANEOUS GSRs FOR NONMEDITATORS
(Katkin, 1965); MEAN NUMBER OF SPONTANEOUS GSRs FOR
NONMEDITATORS AND MEDITATORS (Orme–Johnson, 1971)

results indicate that the frequency of occurrence of spontaneous GSRs is less for meditators than for nonmeditators. Orme-Johnson inferred, therefore, that the meditators had less internal stress than did the nonmeditators. (See Orme-Johnson's paper in Psychosomatic Medicine, Vol. 35, No. 4, 1973.)

3. Tests of Sensory Perception

Eight subjects participated in an experiment (Graham, 1971) to test the hypothesis "that the regular practice of Transcendental Meditation will tend to progressively lower the perceptual thresholds." This experiment was undertaken to scientifically evaluate the many subjective reports of improved perception by TM practitioners.

Four subjects were tested before and after meditating for 20 minutes, and 3 to 10 days later were retested before and after reading a book for 20 minutes. Four other subjects were first tested before and after reading a book, and 3 to 10 days later were tested before and after meditating. A modified "warble" technique was used to determine the acoustical frequency and amplitude discrimination thresholds. The right and left ears were tested monaurally initially, then binaurally.

Graham notes that "there was a greater improvement (i.e., a drop in threshold) after meditating for twenty minutes than after reading a book for twenty minutes and the differences were significant..." Graham (communication to D. P. Kanellakos, 1972) speculated that: "It is possible that psychological factors such as attention could account for significant changes at threshold levels. Another possibility is that neural changes are occurring in the auditory nerves or the auditory cortex... Another possibility is that the lowering of the threshold after meditation is due to a lowering of the neural noise (random firing of neurons in the brain) and the subsequent modification of Weber's Law."

In passing, it may be noted that laboratories at Cambridge and Bristol Universities in England are conducting several studies to discern whether improved discrimination in other sensory modalities may be found as a result of meditation. [See also Pirot (1973), p. 86.]

B. Paper and Pencil Psychological Tests

Seeman et al. (1972) of the University of Cincinnati administered Shostrom's Personality Orientation Inventory (POI) to a group of 35 subjects two days before 15 of them were initiated into TM. (The POI purports to measure "self-actualization.") Two months later, all 35 subjects were retested. These investigators found statistically significant differences between the experimental and control groups for six of the 12 subscales of the POI. For example, the mean difference (between scores obtained during the first and second administration of the test) of the meditation group for the Support Ratio (the Other-Directed versus the Inner-Directed scale) was significantly higher than the mean difference of the nonmeditation (control) group. This ratio measures autonomy, individuality, freedom and confidence. The mean differences obtained for the "Self-Actualizing Value" and "Capacity for Intimate Contact" subscales were also statistically significant.

Maslow (1970, p. 157) stated "...that self-actualizing people can all be described as relatively spontaneous in behavior and far more spontaneous than (those not self-actualized) in their life, thoughts, impulses, etc." Maslow (1968) feels that the self-actualized person tends to live in terms of his wants, likes, dislikes and values and is more self-sufficient, assertive, and affirming.

The results of Seeman's study suggest that, at least in this group of subjects, two months of TM improved their "mental outlook" in comparison with people not practicing TM. The durability of the reported changes is yet to be determined. (See Appendix A, pp. 60,70,72, and 74.)

Similar results were reported by Shelly (1971). Based on a study of 160 practitioners of TM and 145 nonmeditators of similar age and background, he concluded that: "Compared with nonmeditators, meditators (1) are happier and more relaxed; (2) experience the feeling of enjoyment oftener; (3) seek social contacts just as often, yet tend to spend more time alone; (4) develop deeper personal relationships and depend less on their external surroundings for happiness; (5) seek emotional arousal just as often--for example, by engaging in new activities--but tend to avoid extremes of arousal." (See also Appendix A, p. 76.)

Psychologists at the University of Cologne have investigated the psychological characteristics of 49 teachers of TM. The study was undertaken during a congress of teachers of TM in Bremen, Germany, at the Academy of the International Meditation Society, in August 1971 (Fehr et al., 1971). The Freiburger Personality Inventory, which consists of 212 items, was administered to the TM teachers, and their mean scores were compared with normalized standard scores. The results are summarized in Table 2 (see Fehr, p. 91, in Appendix A, Section I.C. for details).

Fehr et al. (1971) reported that teachers of TM:

"(1) have greater psychological stability than the norm.
 (2) are more harmonious and balanced than the norm.
 (3) are more alert in activity than the norm."

They concluded that the observed differences between the subjects and the norm resulted from the practice of TM.

This study was followed by an investigation of an additional 1,000 meditators at the International Teacher Training Course held in Kossen, Austria in October 1971. The data obtained are in the process of being evaluated. [See Fehr in Kniffki, 1974, No. 16 January 1974, pp. 1-9, Ref. listed on p. 139, this book.]

Table 2

AVERAGE DIFFERENCE IN STANDARD DEVIATION UNITS
BETWEEN NORMS (mean = 0) AND TM TEACHERS
(Freiburger Personality Inventory)

Personality Characteristic	Standard Deviations
Nervousness	-0.95
Aggression	-0.33
Depression	-0.86
Irritability	-0.98
Sociability	+0.63
Self-assuredness	+0.77
Tendency to dominate	-0.11
Inhibition	-0.94
Self-criticism	-0.28
Outgoingness	+0.24
Emotional instability	-0.93
Staying power and efficiency	+1.02

Similar positive psychological effects have been reported by other investigators. For example, Doucette (1972) reported that meditation had a significant influence in lowering tension and anxiety levels in student meditators as compared to two groups of nonmeditators. Boese and Berger (1972) reported meditators to have significantly less verbalizations of hostility in the Thematic Apperception Test.

C. Drug Abuse

The available evidence suggests that practice of TM results in some positive physiological and psychological effects. One positive psychophysiological effect--if the initial findings are upheld by more carefully controlled studies--could have great social significance. This effect is the reported reduction in the use of illicit drugs. Three studies, mainly retrospective, are described below. (See also Appendix A, pp. 98-103.)

1. Harvard University Study

Benson and Wallace (1971) administered questionnaires about the use of nonprescribed drugs, alcohol, and cigarettes to approximately 1,950 meditators who had been practicing TM for three months or longer and were attending a month-long teacher-training course in TM. Of the 1,862 questionnaires completed, approximately 58 percent were from males and 42 percent from females. About 50 percent of the respondents were between 19 and 23 years of age, with an overall range of 14 to 78 years.

Within three months of beginning practice of TM, as shown in Figure 10, a vast majority of the practitioners of TM reported a marked decrease in their use of drugs in all categories. The number of subjects using drugs progressively decreased as the duration of practice increased. Most of the subjects who had practiced for 21 months reported that they had almost completely stopped using drugs. For example, in the six-month period before starting TM, about 80 percent of the subjects used marijuana, and of those, 23 percent were heavy users.* After practicing TM for six months, 37 percent used marijuana and of those, only 6.8 percent were heavy users. The reported decrease in abuse of LSD was even more marked. Similar results were found with the other drugs. Reported decreases in the use of alcohol and tobacco were not as dramatic as with the other categories of drugs; yet the trend suggests decreased use.

Of the 20 percent of the subjects who sold drugs before starting TM, about 72 percent stopped and about 12 percent decreased selling during the first three months after instruction. Among the subjects who practiced TM 21 months or longer, about 96 percent stopped selling drugs.

2.   Stanford Research Institute Study

A preliminary analysis of some data obtained in one study conducted by Stanford Research Institute (Otis, 1972) tends to corroborate the findings of Wallace (1970b) and Benson and Wallace (1971) with respect to claims made by TM practitioners that they discontinue drugs after starting TM; the results, however, were related to the degree to which individuals are committed to TM.

Questionnaires soliciting information about selected physical and behavioral symptoms (Otis Physical and Behavioral Inventory: Form A) and an adjective check list (Otis Descriptive Personality List: Form A) were distributed to approximately 900 persons practicing TM who attended a one-month course at the Humboldt State College, Arcata, California, in August 1971. The purpose of the course, sponsored by the Students' International Meditation Society, was to qualify TM practitioners to become

---

*Heavy use for all categories, except LSD and other hallucinogens, means more than once a day, medium use is once a day, and light use is less than once a day. In the case of LSD, more than once a week was called heavy use; less than once a week, medium use; and once a month, light use.

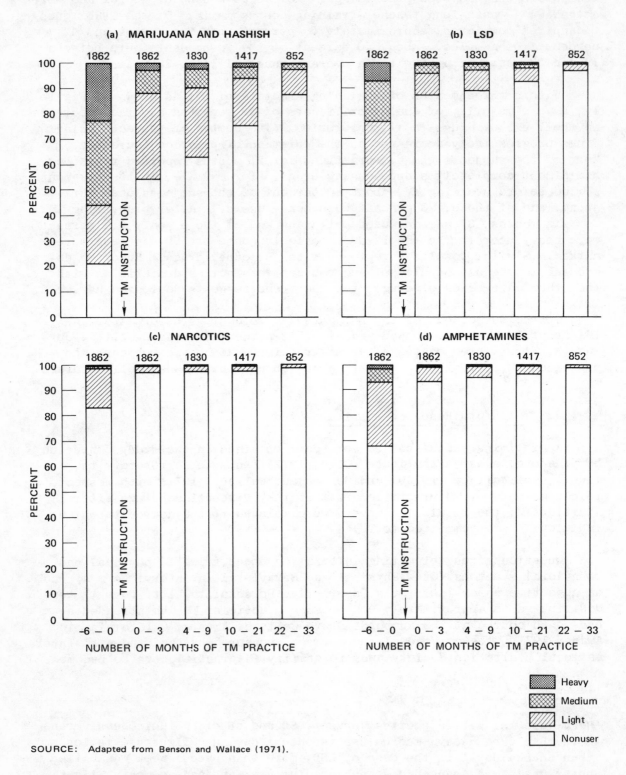

SOURCE: Adapted from Benson and Wallace (1971).

FIGURE 10   REPORTED CHANGES IN USE OF VARIOUS CATEGORIES OF NONPRESCRIBED
DRUGS AS A FUNCTION OF NUMBER OF MONTHS OF TM PRACTICE

teachers of TM. The questionnaires and adjective check lists were distributed at the end of the one-month course. Of the 900 people who were given the two forms, 570 returned both and 620 returned the Physical and Behavioral Inventory, which contained a section on the use of drugs.

The data reported are from the drug-use section of the Physical and Behavioral Inventory only. Of the 620 respondees, 396 reported that they had used drugs, and 84% of these reported that they had given up drugs after starting meditation. Forty-two of them were of a group of 49 opiate users. In a similar study on a random sample of TM practitioners on the mailing list of SIMS, Los Angeles, the results were less impressive but still significant. Of 199 practitioners who had used drugs, 109 (57%) claimed that they had completely given up drugs after starting TM. Seven of 10 opiate users made the same claim. In the two studies, 53 persons claimed that TM either was without effect on their drug use habits (N = 34) or increased their use of drugs (N = 19). Of 51 drug users who had stopped practicing TM (SIMS study), only 21.5% indicated that they had completely stopped using drugs; 31.3% claimed that their drug use had not changed, and 25.4% claimed that it had increased. Nevertheless, the overwhelming effect was a decrease in drug use by people who took up TM and continued its practice. The difference between the results of the Humboldt and SIMS studies in the percentage of people who gave up drugs suggests that personal commitment to TM and motivation to give up drugs are important variables. The Humboldt group consisted of TM practitioners who are being trained to become teachers; the SIMS group consisted of people from all walks of life who have simply been trained in TM.

Otis (1972) points out that the interpretation of these changes in drug use habits is difficult for the following reasons. First, the changes reported were retrospective and their validity depended on accurate recall. Second, the large changes in drug use patterns previously reported by Winquist (1969) and Benson and Wallace (1971) were known to the Humboldt group. Accordingly, they may have been biased toward reporting, or at least exaggerating, changes in their own drug use habits. Contraindicating this possibility was the finding that some of the subjects reported no effects of TM or an increase in their drug use after starting TM. Also, since the degree of drug dependence was not investigated, it may be that only those who used drugs infrequently and experimentally found changes in their drug use habits. This is doubtful, however, since 96% of those who claimed to have given up drugs also stated that drug use "was a problem" for them before they started TM. Nevertheless, since SIMS requires that people desiring to take up TM refrain from any nonprescribed drug use for at least two weeks prior to starting training in TM, strong dependency is contraindicated. It is also possible that drugs are discontinued before people start TM and that the actual practice of TM may have little or nothing to do with stopping drug use; at best, TM may only help to sustain the drug user's resolve to discontinue drugs.

Otis' data are consistent with Winquist's (1969) original findings. Prior to the latter's study, there was no known claim by teachers of TM that drug use would be markedly affected by practicing TM. (See Otis, Appendix D, p. 140.)

3.   City Hospital, Malmo, Sweden

As indicated above, most studies of the effects of TM on drug usage
are retrospective, depending heavily on recall, and the course of changes
in drug use patterns with time of practicing meditation is not directly
observable. One study that controls for some of these methodological
problems is that conducted by Bräutigam (1971).

She solicited the participation of known users (known through treatment for hepatitis) of hashish and "hard" drugs (LSD, amphetamines, and
opiates), most of whom had been convicted of drug use offenses. The 20
users were divided randomly into an experimental group, which was taught
TM, and a control group, which was engaged in group counseling about as
frequently as the experimental group was engaged in training in TM and
"checking." Both groups were subdivided into users of "hard" drugs (LSD,
amphetamines, opiates) and "light" drugs (hashish only). Apparently,
all the subjects had used the hard drugs at least 10 times in the six
months preceding the study. On the average, users of hashish in both
groups had used it about 20 times in the month preceding the study.

After three months of practicing TM, the experimental subjects had
reduced their use of hashish to about three times per month per person;
within six months, however, drug use had increased to six times per month
per individual. The control subjects, in contrast, were using hashish
about 18 times per month per person.

In the month before the study began, use of "hard" drugs was about
three times per month per individual in both the control and experimental
groups. After three months, the meditators were using hard drugs about
0.2 times per month per subject, on the average, while the control group
increased drug use to about seven times per month per subject. After
six months of meditation, use of "hard" drugs had increased to about 0.8
times per month per subject. (See also Appendix A, pp. 99-100.)

D.   Perceived Mental and Physical Health

1.   A Study at UCLA

Wallace (1970b) analyzed a set of questionnaires dealing with the
physical and mental health of a group of meditators attending some
courses and meetings conducted by the Students International Meditation
Society. Of 394 subjects who answered the questionnaire, 67 percent reported improvements in physical health (including reductions in high
blood pressure; reduced frequency of attacks of ulcers, asthma, epilepsy,
and allergies; fewer headaches and colds; and decreased physical tensions).
Eighty-four percent of the respondees reported improvements in mental
health, and three percent reported no noticeable changes in physical
health. With respect to mental health, 22 subjects (of the 272 reporting an improvement) stated that they were no longer under regular
psychiatric treatment, and 25 reported less severe attacks of depression

and fewer suicidal urges. It appears evident from these data that individuals who take up TM feel that they derive some important subjective benefits from its practice. The duration of such effects, however, is unknown at present.

2.   SRI Study at Humboldt State College

Fourteen items from the 30-item behavioral portion of the Otis Physical and Behavioral Inventory (Form A) were preselected by Dr. Joseph McPherson (Senior Behavioral Scientist at SRI) as being consistent with creativity. In addition, two specific questions dealt with the subjects' perceived state of mental health and the extent to which they were receiving psychological or psychiatric help. Of the 620 questionnaires returned by practitioners of TM after a training course at Humboldt State College, 216 were randomly selected for detailed analysis. The responses of these subjects were analyzed to determine if the reported changes were in the direction predicted as consistent with creativity.

McPherson (personal communication to D. Kanellakos) suggests that increased creativity is compatible with reported increases of most of the behavioral characteristics listed in Table 3. The exceptions are Nos. 1, 3, 8, 12, 14, and 16. For these items, decreases suggest increased creativity. It will be noted in the table that the reported changes in behavior were generally consistent with those predicted as indicating increased creativity. For example, of the 101 people who thought restlessness was a problem for them before beginning TM, about 56 percent reported a considerable or complete decrease in restlessness after learning and practicing TM. In contrast, only about 9 percent reported a considerable or complete increase in restlessness after practicing TM for some time.

Although the vast majority of the respondents reported positive changes, certain negative changes were reported. For example, of the 93 individuals who reported "antisocial behavior" as being a problem before beginning TM, about 23 percent reported an increase in this behavior after beginning TM. In general, about one-fourth of the subjects who reported that problems existed before beginning TM reported them to be exacerbated after practicing TM; there were, however, very few reports of complete change for the worse in any category.

Before TM, 15 percent of the subjects reported a need for psychiatric help, and 30 percent felt that they had a mental health problem. The marked decrease in dependence on psychiatric help and the reported marked self-improvement in overall mental health after practicing TM may be important findings for this group. An interesting speculation is that concern about mental health may have been a significant factor in motivating these subjects to take up TM. Many individuals apparently begin TM to solve some problem and apparently feel that they derive

Table 3

NUMBER OF SUBJECTS REPORTING BEHAVIORAL CHANGES
CONSISTENT WITH INCREASED CREATIVITY AFTER STARTING TM

Item No.	BEFORE TM Was a Problem For Me	Behavior or Perceived Attribute	SINCE STARTING TM						
			Little or No Change (0-25%)	Some Change (26-50%)		Considerable Change (51-90%)		Complete Change (91-100%)	
				Incr.	Decr.	Incr.	Decr.	Incr.	Decr.
1	93*	Antisocial behavior	9*	9	23**	9	19	3	21
2	91	Awareness	8	15	2	36	6	22	2
3	105	Boredom	11	2	29	3	42	2	16
4	112	Energy level	19	25	2	43	1	22	0
5	126	Enjoyment of life	6	20	2	45	0	51	2
6	42	Intuitive insights	5	16	0	12	1	8	0
7	84	Productivity	12	20	2	33	3	14	0
8	101	Restlessness	10	4	22	6	37	3	19
9	149	Self-confidence	11	34	3	67	0	32	2
10	106	Self-love	8	31	1	42	0	23	1
11	112	Self-understanding	6	29	2	43	1	29	2
12	78	Suspiciousness of others	9	2	17	4	29	1	16
13	107	Tolerance of others	11	18	1	49	4	22	2
14	95	Withdrawal	15	5	21	2	35	3	14
15	68	General mental health	4	11	0	31	0	21	1
16	33	Psychiatric help	3	1	2	1	2	2	22

*Number of respondees.
**Underlined numbers are in the predicted direction.

36

considerable benefits from TM, as is illustrated by some testimonials collected by SIMS or sent as unsolicited correspondence to D. Kanellakos (see Appendix C).

Editor's Note:

Additional material about perceived and objectively verified improvements of physical and mental health has appeared since the publication of the original SRI report. Some of the references on this subject can be found in Benson and Wallace on reduced hypertension (p. 59), in Wilson and Hornsberger on reduced symptoms of asthma (p. 64); about reduced anxiety in prison populations by Ballou, p. 66; Cunningham and Koch, p. 69; and Orme-Johnson, p. 82; on student health (Ferguson and Gowan, p. 72); on improved performance in business (Frew, p. 73); students' grades (Collier, p. 68; Heaton and Orme-Johnson, p. 74); about reduction of dental inflammation (Klemons, p. 74); on rapid recovery from REM deprivation (Miskiman, p. 80); on insomnia (Miskiman, p. 80); on visual and auditory perceptual acuity (Pelletier, p. 85; Pirot, p. 86); on helping psychiatric patients (Stroebel, p. 87; Glueck, p. 92), and drug abuse (pp. 98-103).

IV ARE THERE ANY DELETERIOUS EFFECTS OF TM PRACTICE?

Data obtained in several recent studies (see Sections II and III and Appendix A) indicate that beneficial physical, mental and social effects are widely claimed by practitioners of TM. However, some observers have questioned the uniformly positive effects that tend to be reported. This section is addressed to the question of whether there are any harmful or negative effects resulting from practicing TM.

Because of the absence of literature in this area, Maharishi Mahesh Yogi was asked to comment regarding possible deleterious effects resulting from the practice of various forms of meditation. He has responded as follows: "It is commonly understood that people who take to the meditative life, like monks, become introverted and avoid activity; they don't seem to participate in the progress of civilization. The tendency of this type of life shows the deleterious effects on the physiology of its practitioners. Such people, who use these wrong systems of meditation, neither contribute their best to society nor do they derive the joy of life from the advances made in civilization. This is the deleterious effect of those types of meditation. In contrast, the physiological changes brought about through TM energize the system, as is clear from Wallace, Orme-Johnson, and others."

According to Maharishi Mahesh Yogi, TM results in stress release or "normalization" of the nervous system. Although he recognizes that there are other efficient ways of removing stress, he teaches that TM is more efficient than either deep sleep or dreaming in removing certain types of stress--those that have accumulated (or have been "stored") in the central nervous system. Such release of stress, however, may have some transient unpleasant consequences--almost always in a mild form.

It has been theorized (Maharishi Mahesh Yogi, 1966; Goleman, 1971) that the physiological and biochemical changes that accompany the TM process relieve the nervous system of strain and stresses located at "deeper levels" (Freud's unconscious?) than those reached during either deep sleep or the dream state. Maharishi suggests that when TM becomes a self-induced biological rhythm or cycle, it tends to "purify" the nervous system, enabling man to become aware of pure "being or existence" and thus to develop his "creative intelligence." The TM process is compared to the processes that take place when the biological cycles of the sleep-dream periods rejuvenate the mind and body, permitting increased physiological and mental efficiency (Hartman, 1967), but TM presumably operates on systems that are not affected by sleep and dreaming.

Maharishi (1966) has proposed that certain physiological and biochemical changes accompany this process of restoring or "balancing" the nervous system. After practicing TM regularly (morning and evening), the body eventually may become accustomed to new physiological rhythms. Accordingly, stopping the practice of TM may introduce some "roughness" into the life of the person who has previously practiced it regularly. [Apparently, "roughness" relates to feelings similar to those experienced when one's regular rest and activity cycle is distorted, as, for example, by time zone changes ("jet lag") or by changes in sleeping habits.] This roughness is assumed to eventually subside and the individual restabilizes his physiological rhythms at premeditation levels. Some individuals may consider this roughness as being "deleterious." To avoid it, Maharishi indicates that one has only to practice TM regularly, just as one must sleep regularly to avoid fatigue.

A.   TM and Release of Stress

As the hypothetical stresses are released during TM, they are assumed to give rise to a variety of phenomena (i.e., thoughts, feelings, sensations) similar to those that occur during dreaming. These mental phenomena may be experienced with positive or negative affect, i.e., heaviness, warmth, floating or falling, pain, etc. Luthe (1970, Vol. V, p. 7), one of the chief proponents of autogenic training, states that during such training: "Intensive feelings of warmth are usually reported after particularly disturbing subjective material has been released and significant progress in brain-desired directions has been made." Some of the phenomena described by Luthe may resemble those observed in a psychiatrist's office during the psychotherapeutic processes and may at times be experienced during meditation. The difference, however, between TM and psychoanalysis appears to be that the latter aims at releasing the "repressed" accumulated stress or "blocked" experiences. In TM, on the other hand, Maharishi teaches that the "mind" itself is strengthened by means of the deep rest to the nervous system occurring during TM practice, and the negative effects of the release of stress are minimized (Vanselow, 1968). In this context, Goleman (1971) considers TM to be a much deeper process than psychoanalysis.

In a private communication to D. Kanellakos (1972), Maharishi stated: "The mind is stronger when it is experiencing very refined states of mental activity. At such times it is very powerful and does not experience the impact of the release of stress with the same intensity with which it experienced the original impact; thus, this influence is greatly diluted. The quality of the mental and physical sensations of this release of stress depends upon the quality of the stress which is being released. In addition, the coherent nature of the impulses of stress release depends upon whether one stress or many are being released at the same time. This will depend on the coherent nature of perception. For example, in a dream we may see a man jump off a cliff, but he may become a tiger or monkey before he reaches the bottom or he may begin to float up in the middle of the fall. This shows release of the stress of a number of experiences, i.e., one could release one or many or parts of many stresses at a time. This obviously dilutes the effect of the original experience.

In psychoanalysis, the aim is to relive the experience in order to become free of symptoms produced by its exclusion from awareness and to allow repressed areas of the personality to once again participate in the conscious life of the individual. Psychoanalysis and related techniques are severely limited in their effectiveness by the fact that they do not include any means of simultaneously strengthening the mind and nervous system. These experimental attempts at improved integration are laudable in intent; however, they are proceeding on the basis of present weakness of the system and the results are therefore limited at best and can be undesirable."

Meditators typically report that the normalizing phenomena of TM are of short duration, usually a few seconds, and only after the fact does one realize that a certain symptom--due presumably to some deep-seated, unconscious stress--has disappeared or has been reduced in severity. At certain other times, however, when a "large block" of stress is being "dissolved," the unstressing phenomena may last a few minutes. If such a stress release takes place at the end of the meditation period and the meditation period is ended abruptly, psychological distress may be experienced for up to several hours afterwards. If such occurrences persist, it is suggested that the meditator consult his teacher, who has been trained to cope with such problems.

Special instructions are given to novice meditators on how to handle situations of continued release of stress. Those who do not follow the instructions, or forget to apply them, may report that meditation has a disagreeable, negative, or deleterious effect. After a few weeks or months of TM practice, however, the meditator usually becomes familiar with such occurrences and learns how to handle them. Essentially, he deals with them as he does with dreams; the meditator learns not to analyze them during meditation but to continue the process of meditation uncritically until it is over. At the termination of meditation, feelings of relief and satisfaction are typical and these tend to reduce the negative effects felt during the normalizing process of meditation, whenever it occurs.

B.   SRI Study

Some negative effects of meditation were noted during the course of a pilot study at Stanford Research Institute.

This study, which spanned about 15 months, involved 60 volunteer employees or adult members of their families, half of whom were randomly selected for training in TM, with the remaining half serving in control groups. One control group mimicked the TM procedure by repeating an English phrase* during their two daily meditation periods; the second control group sat quietly twice a day but did not repeat any phrase; the third did not change their life style in any way, but were given physiological and psychological pre- and post-tests, as were all subjects in the experiment. The experimental (TM) subjects and the first

_____
*   The phrase was "I am a witness only."

two control groups were required to fill out daily logs to record the frequency and duration of their meditation periods. Frequent personal and group contacts were used to sustain motivation.

About three months after beginning the study, the 55 subjects remaining in the experiment were interviewed for one-half hour, using a specific format.* Each subject was questioned regarding his predisposition toward TM (positive, negative, neutral or skeptical) before the experiment started; his expectations as a participant, whether he was "looking for something" that could be of personal value when the experiment started; whether he would have gone into TM on his own if there had been no experiment (all subjects, irrespective of their group assignment, had been exposed to one or two introductory lectures on TM); and other similar questions. They were also asked what physiological or psychological effects (i.e., none, positive or negative) they may have experienced, and to state what they were.

A preliminary analysis of the interview data was undertaken for purposes of this review. Plus, minus and zero scores (ranging from -5 to +5 for each question) were assigned to the various questions involving level of motivation and predisposition toward TM in order to derive a summed score for this variable. Plus, minus, or zero scores (also having a range of -5 to +5) were given for any effects mentioned, depending on whether they were interpreted by the subject as positive, negative, or of no consequence, to derive a summed score for "Effects."

The "Effects" data are summarized in Figure 11. Of the 28 TM subjects, 22 derived some positive benefits after three months of TM practice, whereas only 10 of the 27 subjects serving in one of the three control conditions claimed any benefits. This difference is statistically significant ($X^2 = 9.746$, $.01 < p > .001$, two-tailed test). Of the 28 TM subjects, 26 indicated that they intended to continue their practice of TM even though the experiment was about to be terminated,** whereas only 5 of the 15 active controls indicated that they had derived sufficient benefits from the control procedures to continue them after the experiment was completed.

About two-thirds (19 out of 28) of those in the TM group made one or more unfavorable remarks about TM during the interview. Their positive remarks are lengthy and varied but, in general, the most favorable ones resemble those reported in Appendix C. Here are some typical

---

*It is recognized that the validity of retrospective interviews can be subject to question; recall may be tempered by forgetting or by trying to please the experimenter.

**The experiment was subsequently continued for another year.

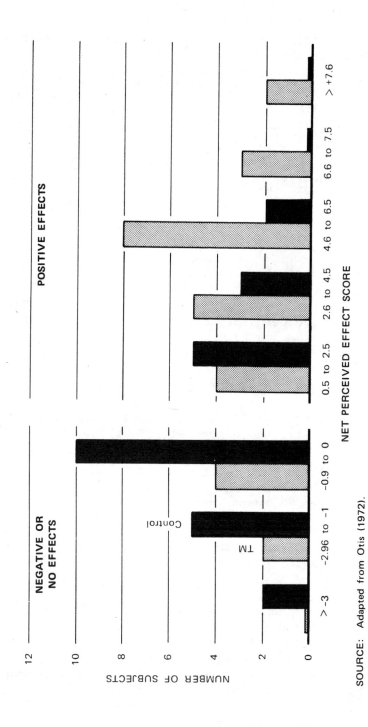

SOURCE: Adapted from Otis (1972).

FIGURE 11   PERCEIVED EFFECTS AFTER THREE MONTHS OF TM PRACTICE

43

examples of "unfavorable" or "negative" remarks made by the SRI subjects after three months of practicing TM:

"I am getting hungry at odd times."

"Occasional insomnia...waking up early."

"I find it distressing and I cannot relax during morning meditation, but okay at noon."

"I resent the mantra; it may be in conflict with my religion."

"When I first started TM, I had some physical symptoms around the front of my head, like when you blow your nose when you have a cold and you open up; it was unpleasant."

"I am disturbed that now alcohol does not make me high. I like to drink."

"I gained a few pounds in the beginning. I changed food habits and am at my regular weight now."

"Eyesight seems to have deteriorated. Can't see at a distance."

"I had a sensation of falling during TM a few times; I was scared."

"I got terrific stomach cramps during TM."

"I had a couple of months of flu and have been extremely fatigued. It was diagnosed as bronchitis and a general infection. It started one months after I started TM. I am more irritable and interpersonal relationships have deteriorated."

"Sometimes I feel more mentally confused."

"I had a period during the first few weeks when I was extremely tired. Dragged all day. Collapsed in bed. Still getting same amount of sleep. TM instructor said this was stress release. Slowly this disappeared."

Most of these remarks appear to be related to what Maharishi (1966) calls "normalizing." Such negative effects are thought to be the physical manifestations of the release of stored-up stress in the nervous system. Like dreams, they are also presumed to be transitory. Experience (with the help of the TM instructor) teaches the novice meditator that such effects may be "normal" during TM, and eventually the psychological or physiological events that occur during meditation are taken in stride. However, there are no systematic data regarding the duration or longevity of the reported negative effects; it is possible that some people may have long-term effects.

The technique of meditation eventually becomes an integral part of the meditator's life; to an outsider, its practice may appear to be a compulsive habit. However, the meditator may at any time choose to discontinue the practice without any apparent long-lasting ill effects. The Students International Meditation Society has estimated that approximately 35 percent of those who start TM voluntarily terminate the practice (personal communication), but about 30 percent of these dropouts start meditating again. Thus, the SIMS dropout frequency approximates 25 percent. The dropout frequency of subjects in the SRI study (46 percent after about six months) was about double the SIMS frequency, presumably because they represented a less motivated population than those that voluntarily take up TM through normal channels.

Approximately six months after the experimental and control conditions were assigned, a telephone survey of all the subjects in the SRI experiment (except those six control subjects who chose not to take up TM at the end of the test period) was conducted. The purpose was to determine the regularity of practice and the reasons dropouts stopped their practice of TM. Two to four minutes were spent on the telephone with each subject. Those in the original TM groups had been meditating about six months and those serving as controls initially had been meditating for about three months.

This survey revealed that 23 subjects (46 percent) had either stopped (19 subjects) or were meditating only a few times a week (4 subjects). Four subjects were meditating regularly, but only once a day. The remaining 27 subjects were meditating regularly twice a day.

The most common reasons for stopping the practice of TM were, in rank order, (1) lack of time in a busy schedule, (2) no subjectively perceived benefits, and (3) interference of the procedure with present habits or style of life. Those who stopped apparently did so without any ill effects.

Those who were meditating regularly once a day claimed that they continued to derive some benefits. As compared with once-a-day meditators, almost all of those who were meditating regularly twice a day were quite explicit in describing major benefits from its practice; it is difficult, however, to ascertain on the basis of this interview the extent of the differences in benefits claimed by those meditating once a day as opposed to those meditating twice daily. Differential effects based on frequency, duration and periodicity of meditation is a question for future research to determine.

Also requiring future research is the question of possible long-term deleterious effects that may occur, especially in unstable individuals who take up the practice of TM. It will be recalled that Otis (1972) found that TM resulted in an increase in drug abuse in some individuals and that approximately 23% of the Humboldt population of regular meditators reported an increase in their antisocial behavior. Thirty percent of this population also felt that they had a mental health problem before starting TM.

V SUMMARY AND CONCLUSIONS

A number of papers (many unpublished and many based on pilot or preliminary experiments of poor or questionable design) have reported various physiological, biochemical and psychological variables associated with the practice of Transcendental Meditation (TM) in both novice and seasoned meditators. Taken at face value, the data gathered thus far appear to suggest that some consistent and characteristic psychobiological effects accompany the practice of TM. But these are apparently shared by some of the other meditation techniques. Sometimes these are evident, particularly in seasoned meditators, outside of the meditation session itself. These psychobiological effects appear to differ, at least in certain important respects, from those associated with wakefulness, dreaming, and deep sleep, and have been assumed to define a "transcendental state of consciousness," or TC-state.* The TC-state is presumably characterized by a wakeful alert brain; a marked reduction or absence of voluntary thought processes; a low metabolic rate; reduced autonomic reactivity; and deep relaxation of the somatic musculature. Among other subjective feelings, practitioners typically report a deep sense of well-being and feelings of "peace within oneself." A respectable percentage (about 20%) also report the amelioration or complete disappearance of various physical and psychological symptoms typically associated with psychosomatic illnesses. A large majority of drug users who take up TM typically report discontinuing drugs after starting the practice of the technique, but whether or not drugs are discontinued appears to relate to the individual's commitment to the practice and philosophy of TM.

The degree to which the psychobiological effects reported for TM may have features in common with effects produced by other techniques of deep relaxation (including yogi, Zen, progressive relaxation, autogenic training and biofeedback) and the reliability of the reported effects remain to be determined by further research.

Also, the degree to which TM may represent a technique for the wakeful induction and maintenance of Sleep Stage 1--with which it appears to share a number of common characteristics--is not known and represents a fertile area for further investigation.

Finally, the possibility of long-term deleterious effects from the practice of TM, especially in unstable individuals, should be investigated.

---

*Hypothesizing such a state at this stage of our knowledge may have heuristic value.

REFERENCES CITED IN TEXT

Y. Akishige. A historical survey of the psychological studies in Zen. Kyushu Psychol. Stud. 5, Bull. Fac. Lit. Kyushu Univ. 11, 1-56 (1968).

J. Allison. Respiratory changes during Transcendental Meditation. Lancet, No. 7651, 833-834 (18 April 1970).

B. K. Anand, G. S. China and B. Singh. Some aspects of electroencephalographic studies in Yogis. Electroencephalog. Clin. Neurophysiol. 13, 452-456 (1961).

Anonymous. TM, Some Results. Students International Meditation Society, 1015 Gayley Avenue, Los Angeles, California, 1969.

B. K. Bagchi and M. A. Wenger. Electro-physiological correlates of some Yogi exercises. Electroencephalog. Clin. Neurophysiol., Suppl. 7, 132-149 (1957).

H. Benson and R. K. Wallace. Decreased drug abuse with Transcendental Meditation: A study of 1862 subjects. In Proceedings of Drug Abuse, International Symposium for Physicians, University of Michigan, Ann Arbor, Michigan, November 10-13, 1970. Lea and Febinger, Philadelphia, 1972. Also printed in Congressional Record, Hearings Before the Select Committee on Crime, House of Representatives, 92nd Congress, First Session, June 2, 3, 4, and 23, 1971. Serial No. 92-1, U.S. Government Printing Office, Washington, D.C., 1971.

K. Blasdell. The effect of Transcendental Meditation on a perceptual motor task. Submitted in partial fulfillment of the requirements for the M.S. degree, Department of Psychology, University of California at Los Angeles, California, December 1971.

E. Boese and K. Berger. In search of a fourth state of consciousness: Psychological and physiological correlates of meditation. In press, 1972. (Pennsylvania State Medical School, Hershey, Pa.)

G. Bohlin. Monotonous stimulation, sleep onset and habituation of the orienting reaction. Electroencephalog. Clin. Neurophysiol. 31, 593-601 (1971).

E. Bräutigam. The effect of Transcendental Meditation on drug abusers. Unpublished report, research conducted at City Hospital, Malmö, Sweden, December 1971. (Available from Students' International Meditation Society, Los Angeles, California.)

49

F. M. Brown, W. S. Stuart and J. T. Blodgett. EEG kappa rhythms during Transcendental Meditation and possible perceptual threshold changes following. Presented to Kentucky Academy of Science, Richmond, Kentucky, November 13, 1971 (revised 1972).

N. N. Das and H. Gastaut. Variations de l'activité electrique du cerveau, du coeur et des muscles squelletiques au cours de la meditation et de l'extase Yogique. Electroencephalog. Clin. Neurophysiol., Suppl. 6, 211-219 (1955).

K. K. Datey, S. N. Deshmukh, C. P. Dalvi and S. L. Vinekar. "Shavasan": A yogic exercise in the management of hypertension. Angiology 20, 325-333 (1969).

A. Deikman. Experimental meditation. J. Nervous Mental Disease 136, 329-343 (1963).

A. Deikman. Implications of experimentally produced contemplative meditation. J. Nervous Mental Disease 142, 101-116 (1966a).

A. Deikman. De-automatization and the mystic experience. Psychiatry 29, 324-338 (1966b).

W. C. Dement. The biology of dreaming. Ph.D. thesis, University of Chicago, 1958.

W. Dement. Effect of dream deprivation. Science 131, 1705-1707 (1960).

W. Dement. Eye movements during sleep. In M. Bender, Ed., The Oculomotor System. Harper and Row, New York, 1964, pp. 316-366.

R. S. de Ropp. Self-transcendence and beyond. In R. S. de Ropp, The Master Game. Delacorte Press and George Allen and Unwin Ltd., 1968.

L. C. Doucette. Transcendental Meditation as an anxiety reducing agent. Unpublished paper, McMaster University, Hamilton, Ontario, Canada, January 1972. An abstract may be found in: Treatment: A report of the commission of inquiry into non-medical use of drugs, p. 101. Information Canada, 171 Slater Street, Ottawa, Canada, 1972.

T. Fehr, U. Norstehimer and S. Torber. Untersuchung Praktizienden der Transzendentzen von 49 Meditation mit dem Freiburger Persönlichkeits Inventar. Unpublished paper, 1971.

R. Fischer. A cartography of the ecstatic and meditative states. Science 174, 897-904 (1971).

D. Goleman. Meditation as meta-therapy: Hypotheses toward a proposed fifth state of consciousness. J. Transpersonal Psychol. 3(1), 1-25 (1971).

J. Graham. The effects of Transcendental Meditation upon auditory thresholds--a pilot study. Paper submitted in partial fulfillment of the requirements for the B.Sc. degree in Experimental Psychology, University of Sussex, England, June 1971.

E. Hartman. The Functions of Sleep. Yale University Press, New Haven, Connecticut, 1973.

P. Hauri. Effects of evening activity on early night sleep. Psychophysiology 4, 267-277 (1968).

F. Holl, Department of Physiology, Sporthochschul, Cologne, Germany. Private communication, 1971.

J. Kamiya. Conscious control of brain waves. Psychol. Today 1, 57-60 (1968).

J. Kamiya. Operant control of the EEG alpha rhythm and some of its reported effects on consciousness. In C. Tart, Ed., Altered States of Consciousness. John Wiley & Sons, New York, 1969, pp. 507-517.

P. V. Karambelkar, M. V. Bhole and M. L. Gharote. Effect of yogic asanas on uropepsin excretion. Indian J. Med. Res. 57, 944-947 (1969).

A. Kasamatsu and T. Hirai. An electroencephalographic study on Zen meditation (Zasen). Fol. Psychiat. Neurol. Japan 20, 315-336 (1966).

D. Kleitman. Sleep and Wakefulness, revised and enlarged edition. University of Chicago Press, Chicago, Ill., 1963.

A. Kondo. Intuition in Zen Buddhism. Am. J. Psychoanal. 12, 10-14 (1952).

A. Kondo. Zen in psychotherapy: the virtue of sitting. Chicago Review 12, 57-64 (1958).

S. Krippner. Altered states of consciousness. In J. White, Ed., The Highest State of Consciousness. Doubleday and Co., Inc., Garden City, N. Y., 1972.

G. G. Luce. Current Research on Sleep and Dreams. Publ. No. 1389, Public Health Service, U.S. Dept. of Health, Education and Welfare. U.S. Government Printing Office, Washington, D. C. 20402 (1965).

G. G. Luce. Biological Rhythms in Human and Animal Physiology. Dover Publications, New York, 1971. Originally published under the title Biological Rhythms in Psychiatry and Medicine, Publ. No. 2088, Public Health Service, U.S. Dept. of Health, Education and Welfare (1970).

W. Luthe, Ed. Autogenic Therapy, Vols. I to VI. Grune and Stratton, New York, London, 1969, 1970.

Maharishi Mahesh Yogi. The Science of Being and the Art of Living. International SRM Publications, new revised edition, 1966. (Available at any SIM Center. Also published as a Signet paperback, new edition, 1972.)

Maharishi Mahesh Yogi. Commentary on the Bhagavad-Gita. International SRM Publication, 1967, Chapters 1-6. (Also available in paperback: Book 2913, Penguin Books, Baltimore, Maryland, 1969.)

Maharishi Mahesh Yogi. Private communication, April 1972.

R. B. Malmo. Activation: a neurophysiological dimension. Psychol. Rev. 66, 367-386 (1959).

A. H. Maslow. Toward a Psychology of Being. D. Van Nostrand Co., Inc., Princeton, N. J., 2nd ed., 1968.

A. H. Maslow. Motivation and Personality. Harper and Row, New York, 1970.

E. W. Maupin. Zen Buddhism: a psychological view. J. Consult. Psychol. 26, 362-378 (1962).

E. W. Maupin. Individual differences in response to a Zen meditation exercise. J. Consult. Psychol. 29, 139-145 (1965).

A. Onda. Autogenic training and Zen. In W. Luthe, Ed., Autogenic Training, International Edition. Grune and Stratton, New York, 1965, pp. 251-258.

D. W. Orme-Johnson. Autonomic stability and Transcendental Meditation. In Proceedings of the First International Symposium on the Science of Creative Intelligence, Humboldt State College, Arcata, California, August 1971. Also Psychosomatic Med. 35(4), 341-349 (1973).

I. Oswald. Sleeping and Waking: Physiology and Psychology. Elsevier, Amsterdam, 1962.

L. S. Otis. Changes in drug usage patterns of practitioners of Transcendental Meditation (TM). Unpublished report, Stanford Research Institute, Menlo Park, California, January 1972.

L. S. Otis, D. C. Jones and A. Sjoberg. Studies of blood pressure in practitioners of Transcendental Meditation. Stanford Research Institute, Menlo Park, California. In preparation, 1972.

L. S. Otis, D. P. Kanellakos, J. S. Lukas and A. Vassiliades. The psychophysiology of Transcendental Meditation--a pilot study. Unpublished report, Stanford Research Institute, Menlo Park, California, 1972.

A. Rechtschaffen. Discussion of: W. Dement, Part III, "Research Studies: Dreams and Communication," pp. 162-170. Science and Psychoanalysis, VII, Grune and Stratton, New York, 1964.

A. Rechtschaffen and A. Kales, Eds. A Manual of Standardized Terminology, Techniques and Scoring System for Sleep Stages of Human Subjects. Publ. No. 204, Public Health Service, U.S. Government Printing Office, Washington, D. C., 1968.

H. P. Ritterstaedt. A new effect in infrared radiation of the human skin through Transcendental Meditation. Unpublished manuscript, Dusseldorf, Germany, 1966. (Available from SIMS, Los Angeles, California.)

F. Schmit. Private communication, 1971.

W. Seeman, S. Nidich and T. Banta. A study of the influence of Transcendental Meditation on a measure of self-actualization. J. Couns. Psychol. 19, 184-187 (1972).

R. Shaw and D. Kolb. Private communication, 1971.

M. W. Shelly. The role of TM in the post-industrial society. In Proceedings of the First International Symposium on the Science of Creative Intelligence, Humboldt State College, Arcata, California, August 1971 (in press). Also in Sources of Satisfaction and The Counter Evolution; both books in press, 1973.

F. Snyder. New biology of dreaming. Arch. Gen. Psychiat. 8, 381-391 (1963).

F. Snyder. Autonomic nervous system manifestations during sleep and dreaming. In S. S. Kety, E. V. Evarts and H. L. Williams, Eds., Sleep and Altered States of Consciousness, Proc. Assn. for Research in Nervous and Mental Disease, December 3-4, 1965, New York, N. Y. Williams and Wilkins, Baltimore, Maryland, 1967, Vol. 45, Chapter XX.

F. Snyder. Psychophysiology of human sleep. Clin. Neurosurg. 18, 503-536 (1971).

J. Stoyva and J. Kamiya. Electro-physiological studies of dreaming as a prototype of a new strategy in the study of consciousness. Psychol. Rev. 75, 192-205 (1968).

C. Tart, Ed. Altered States of Consciousness. John Wiley & Sons, New York, 1969.

K. Vanselow. Meditative exercises to eliminate the effects of stress. Hippokrates (Stuttgart) 39, 462-465 (1968).

A. Vassiliadis. Physiological effects of Transcendental Meditation--a longitudinal study. Unpublished report, Stanford Research Institute, Menlo Park, California, 1972.

K. Walker. The supra-conscious state. In Images, p. 10, 1964. Hoffman-La Roche Limited.

R. K. Wallace. Physiological effects of Transcendental Meditation. Science 167, 1751-1754 (1970a).

R. K. Wallace. Physiological effects of Transcendental Meditation: a proposed fourth state of consciousness. Ph.D. Thesis, Physiology Department, University of California at Los Angeles, California, June 1970b.

R. K. Wallace and H. Benson. The physiology of meditation. Sci. Amer. 226(2), 84-90 (1972).

R. K. Wallace, H. Benson and A. F. Wilson. A wakeful hypometabolic physiologic state. Am. J. Physiol. 221, 795-799 (1971).

R. W. Wescott. States of consciousness. In R. W. Wescott, The Divine Animal. Funk and Wagnalls, New York, 1969.

W. T. Winquist. The effect of the regular practice of TM on students involved in the regular use of hallucinogenic and hard drugs. Paper submitted to Sociology class, University of California at Los Angeles, 1969. Available from SIMS, Los Angeles.

Appendix A

ANNOTATED SELECTED BIBLIOGRAPHY

Appendix A

ANNOTATED SELECTED BIBLIOGRAPHY*

I. The Psychobiology of Transcendental Meditation

A. Published Research Papers

1. J. Allison. Respiratory changes during transcendental meditation. Lancet, No. 7651, 833-834 (18 April 1970). Also personal communication, September 1969.

Allison suspended thermistors 1 cm from each nostril and the mouth to measure the respiration rate of a meditator. This technique minimized the problems of dead air (when the breath volume becomes very small) and CO_2 build-up (as when masks are used). The velocity and volume of the air breathed were also measured. Allison used a single subject who read a book for a few minutes, meditated for 30 minutes, and then read some more. Six sessions were recorded.

In those sessions when the respiration rate and volume changed within a minute or two after beginning TM, the subject assessed the meditation session as "good." The rate dropped from an average of about 12 per minute to an average of about 6 per minute. The respiratory volume was also judged visually to have decreased. When meditation stopped and reading began, the rate and volume returned within a few minutes to near premeditation values. When, during meditation, the respiration rate had fallen to about 4 per minute and the volume was low, there was no significant change in the values in the subsequent minutes. Both these points were interpreted by Allison as showing no significant build-up of CO_2 (also see Wallace, Ref. 38 in Section I.B. of Appendix A). When the subject was watching a television program, none of the above changes took place. During the third session, rated by the subject as a "fair" meditation, the changes were similar to those during the "good" session but less pronounced (respiration rate dropped to about 8 per minute). During the fourth session, rated as "poor," there was a significant decrease in the respiration rate (down about 7.5 per minute, from a variable 11 to 19 per minute) but there was also a greater volume of air per breath.

---

*The amount of detail provided in these annotations varies. The most detail is provided for those articles or books thought to be most relevant to the subjects discussed in the body of the report. Many abstracts in this appendix were added after publication of the SRI report, and hence are not discussed in the previous sections.

2. J. P. Banquet. EEG and meditation. Electroencephalog. Clin. Neurophysiol. 33, 454 (1972).

"Computerized spectral analysis was performed on selected channels of the EEG recorded during meditation in 10 subjects (Transcendental Meditation as taught by Maharishi Mahesh Yogi), and compared with a control group. The results were graphed on tri-dimensional charts to display time, amplitude and frequency.

"During meditation there are:

"1. Frequency changes. There is a constant tendency to shift from alpha to slow frequencies, mostly theta and mixed frequencies, sometimes low and medium voltage delta. Relatively high voltage rhythmic beta approximately 20 cycles appears usually mixed with alpha and theta, and with simultaneous disappearance of higher beta frequencies. The dominant alpha usually slows by 1 or 2 cycles. The most outstanding feature of these different frequencies is the repetitive occurrence of large amplitude hypersynchrony with occasional sharp waves superimposed and the swift shift from one frequency to another with brief sequence of alpha, theta, delta and return to alpha.

"2. Form and amplitude. The amplitude of alpha is increased at the end of meditation, and usually is higher than in the control subjects. There are some particular wave forms in and out of meditation, the significance of which is in question.

"3. Variation in time. Continuous alternation of alpha and mixed frequencies is typical. Alpha periods predominate at the beginning of meditation. Low mixed theta and beta different from drowsiness are prominent in deep meditation. Rhythmic higher voltage alpha returns at the end.

"4. Topographical changes. Alternately alpha extends from occipito-parietal to central and frontal areas, or frontal beta diffuses towards posterior regions. There are periods of uniformity of frequency and amplitude from all leads in deep meditation. The tendency of some of these changes is to persist after the end of meditation." (Author's abstract.)

3. J. P. Banquet. Spectral analysis of the EEG in meditation. Electroencephalog. Clin. Neurophysiol. 35, 143-151 (1973).

Spectral analyses and typical EEGs were obtained in a group of subjects (N = 12) during TM and compared with those obtained in a resting, control, group (N = 12).

In meditators, alpha rhythm increased in amplitude, slowed down in frequency and extended to anterior channels at the beginning of meditation. In a second stage of meditation, theta frequencies "different from those of sleep" diffused from frontal to posterior

channels. Short theta periods or longer rhythmic theta trains were
seen. In some meditators, alpha and--more rarely--theta waves per-
sisted in the post-meditation period with subject's eyes open.
Rhythmic amplitude-modulated beta waves were present over the whole
scalp in a third stage (the so-called deep stage) in advanced
subjects.

Synchronization of anterior and posterior channels was the most striking topographical alteration. Alpha rhythms spread from the occipito-
parietal to the anterior channels. Theta and beta frequencies usually
appeared first in the frontal channels, then diffused posteriorly.
Transient asymmetry between right and left hemispheres could occur
in the shifting phase from slow to fast frequencies; beta dominant
activity appeared first in the left hemisphere.

"These self-induced changes during meditation are of special interest
inasmuch as they are not produced by other techniques like autosuggestion and hypnosis (Kasamatsu and Hirai, 1966). Their neurophysiological interpretation could be based on three consistent findings
of the deep meditation state: absence or decrease of EEG reaction to
stimulation, even if the subject perceives external and internal
stimuli; simultaneous persistence of an alert state of consciousness,
allowing the subject to memorize and answer questions; possibility of
voluntary movement without any noticeable modification of the brain
wave pattern of deep meditation. We must deduce, therefore, that
the EEG changes of Transcendental Meditation are independent of the
interaction between the subject and the outer world but produced by
the specific mental activity of the practice." (From the author's
summary.)

4. H. Benson and R. K. Wallace. Decreased blood pressure in hypertensive
    subjects who practiced meditation. Supplement II to Circulation, Vols.
    XLV and XLVI, Oct. 1972. Abstracts of the 45th Scientific Sessions.

"An investigation was designed to test the hypothesis that a mental
practice might lower blood pressure in hypertensive subjects. Systemic arterial blood pressure was measured 1,119 times in 22 hypertensive
subjects over 4 to 63 weeks by means of a Random Zero Sphygmomanometer.
After control measurements were taken, the subjects altered their
behavior by regularly practicing a meditational technique, called
Transcendental Meditation, as taught by Maharishi Mahesh Yogi. Resting control blood pressures, prior to learning and practicing meditation, were 150 ± 17 mm Hg systolic (mean ± one standard deviation)
and 94 ± 9 mm Hg diastolic. After starting the practice of meditation, resting blood pressures, independent of the meditational period,
were 141 ± 11 mm Hg systolic and 88 ± 7 mm Hg diastolic (p < 0.001
for systolic and p < 0.005 for diastolic pressure by paired t test).
The lowered blood pressures were independent of whether the subjects
were taking antihypertensive medications and whether they changed

these medications. Elevated systemic arterial blood pressure may therefore be reduced by the altered behavior of practicing meditation." (Authors' abstract.)

5. L. Bourdeau. Transcendental Meditation and yoga as reciprocal inhibitors. J. Behav. Ther. Exp. Psychiat. <u>3</u>, 97-98 (1972).

"In two cases, one of claustrophobia and the other of profuse respiration, transcendental meditation and yoga were therapeutically successful after attempts with systematic desensitization had yielded only partial alleviation." (Author's abstract.)

6. R. Honsberger and A. F. Wilson. Transcendental Meditation in treating asthma. Respiratory Therapy (J. Inhal. Technology) <u>3</u>(6), 79-80 (November-December 1973).

A somewhat longer paper dealing with the research described below in Wilson and Honsberger (Item 17 in this section).

7. S. Nidich, W. Seeman and T. Dreskin. Influence of Transcendental Meditation: a replication. J. Counsel. Psychol. <u>20</u>, 6, 556-566 (1974).

"Shostram's Personal Orientation Inventory (POI) was administered to the experimental group two days prior to their beginning a program of Transcendental Meditation and readministered 10 weeks later. The control group took the tests during the same period of time with no significant difference on any POI variables on the first administration. For 10 of the 12 POI variables, significant differences between experimental and control subjects appeared in the direction of predicted 'self-actualization.' The study replicated the results of the previous study on the influence of Transcendental Meditation." (See Item 10 in this section.) (Authors' abstract.)

8. S. Nidich, W. Seeman and M. Seibert. Influence of Transcendental Meditation on state anxiety. Submitted for publication.

"A-State Anxiety scale was administered to two groups of students. Six weeks later the anxiety scale was readministered, after Ss were instructed to carry out a demanding task, followed by instructions for the controls to 'sit with eyes closed' and the experimentals to 'begin meditation' for 15 minutes. Results show that TM influences the A-State scale in a positive direction for the meditators ($p < .05$)." (Authors' abstract.)

9. D. W. Orme-Johnson. Autonomic stability and Transcendental Meditation. In Proceedings of the First International Symposium on the Science of Creative Intelligence, Humboldt State College, Arcata, California, August 1971. Also Psychosomatic Med. 35(4), 341-349 (1973).

This study showed that the regular practice of TM produced rapid GSR habituation and low levels of spontaneous GSR. Eight meditators and eight nonmeditators were presented with 100-dB, 0.5-sec, 3000-Hz tones once every 53 seconds, on the average. Meditators habituated in about 11 trials and nonmeditators in 26.1 trials, a statistically significant difference. The waveform of the GSR was found to be more stable for meditators, with fewer "secondary responses" in the recovery limb of the response, than for nonmeditators, and meditators showed fewer spontaneous GSR fluctuations (of 100 ohms or greater) than nonmeditators did. Whereas nonmeditators were normal on spontaneous GSR frequency compared with data in the literature (35 per 10 minutes), meditators were unusually stable (8.71 per 10 minutes).

A second study showed that nonmeditators planning to begin TM obtained normal resting frequencies of spontaneous GSR, and a second group of meditators was, again, found to be unusually stable. By all three criteria of autonomic stability (i.e., rate of habituation, number of secondary responses, and the frequency of spontaneous GRS), meditators showed more stable autonomic nervous systems than nonmeditators did.

It is suggested that regular practice of TM (which presumably induces a wakeful hypometabolic state) stabilizes resting autonomic functions and reduces sympathetic activity, thus deterring psychosomatic disease and maintaining good health. (Adapted from the author's summary.)

10. W. Seeman, S. Nidich and T. Banta. A study of the influence of Transcendental Meditation on a measure of self-actualization. J. Couns. Psychol. 19, 184-187 (1972).

"Shostrom's Personality Orientation Inventory (POI) test was administered to an experimental group (N = 15) two days prior to the beginning of a program of Transcendental Meditation. The control group of nonmeditators (N = 20) took the POI at the same time. Experimental and control subjects did not differ significantly on any of the POI scales on the first administration. Two months later, following regular meditation sessions by the experimental subjects, the POI was again administered to both groups. For six of the twelve POI variables there were differences between experimental and control subjects, and in the direction of predicted 'self-actualization.' The psychological import of these changes was discussed, as were implications for further study." (Authors' abstract.)

11. R. J. Stek and B. A. Bass "Personal adjustment and perceived locus of control among students interested in meditation", <u>Psychological Reports</u>, 32, 1019-1022, (1973).

Selected personality correlates were investigated in four groups of college students. The first group of 13 subjects voluntarily paid for additional instruction (after two free introductory lectures) in TM; the second group of 34 attended at least two introductory lectures about TM but decided not to or were unable to pay for further instruction; an additional 27 students knew the courses were being offered but were not interested in attending them; and the fourth group consisted of 30 randomly selected introductory psychology students.

Three selected personality characteristics were measured by Rotter's Internal-External Control of Reinforcement scale, and by Shostrom's Personality Orientation Inventory. Rotter's test estimated the extent to which the subject perceived the motivation and rewards for his behavior as coming from himself (internal control), while two of Shostrom's scales measured time competency and internal support (these estimate an attribute similar to that estimated by Rotter's internal control).

Stek and Bass found no significant difference between the groups on any of the scales. They conclude that it is unwarranted to assume that college students who are interested in or who pursue TM are either more or less neurotic or self-actualized than their non-interested counterparts.

12. M. Treichel, N. Clinch and M. Cran. The metabolic effects of Transcendental Meditation. The Physiologist <u>16</u>, 472 (1973).

"It is now accepted that mental states alter physiological function. The technique of Transcendental Meditation (TM) has been reported to produce a substantial decrease in oxygen consumption during short test periods (Wallace, Benson and Wilson, Am. J. Physiol. <u>221</u>, 795). We have repeated these experiments using a method designed to reduce interference with the subject's respiration. Fifty-six experiments were run on 15 experienced meditators and a similar series of 36 experiments was made with 15 control subjects. In each case nasal air velocities were measured using heated thermistors, and nasal air was analysed continuously for pCO_2. Each experiment was divided into 3 sections. During the first 20 minutes both groups were instructed to read; during the second period of 20 minutes meditators meditated while the control group sat comfortably and relaxed with closed eyes; during the final 20 minutes both groups were instructed to read. Mean minute volume ($\dot{V}$), minute CO_2 production ($\dot{V}_{CO_2}$), as well as respiratory frequency were computed for each experimental section. Meditation was associated with decreases of $1.6 \pm .2$ liters/min and 71 ± 8 ml/min in $\dot{V}$ and $\dot{V}_{CO_2}$ respectively (means and

S.E. of the means), with no significant change in respiratory frequency. These changes are in the same order of size but slightly larger than those previously reported. However, the tests with non-meditating subjects unexpectedly produced similar results (ΔV 1.3 ± .2 liters/min; ΔV_{CO_2} 45 ± 10 ml/min). We conclude that under the conditions of our experiments, the decrease in metabolic rate achieved by our meditating subjects was not necessarily related to the practice of the technique." (Authors' abstract.)

13. R. K. Wallace. Physiological effects of Transcendental Meditation. Science 167, 1751-1754 (1970).

Wallace studied 15 subjects who had practiced TM from six months to three years. Subjects acted as their own controls during a 1-hour recording session. Subjects sat with their eyes open, then closed, before and after a 20- to 30-minute meditation period.

Total oxygen consumption during TM decreased a maximum of 20% ($p < .001$), but the respiratory quotient (volume of CO_2 eliminated/ O_2 consumed) did not change significantly. Mean heart rate decreased about five beats per minute ($p < .001$) and the mean skin resistance more than doubled ($p < .001$). In the frontal area of the brain, alpha waves (8-12 Hz) increased and theta waves (4-7 Hz) appeared in almost all subjects. Disruption of alpha waves (called alpha blocking) showed no habituation. He concluded that, physiologically, TM is not related to hypnotism or sleep states.

14. R. K. Wallace and H. Benson. The physiology of meditation. Sci. Amer. 226(2), 84-90 (1972).

This is a review article based on their work on the physiology of TM (see Ref. 15 below). The 36 normal subjects used in the study acted as their own controls. The authors describe the TM state as an integrated response of a wakeful hypometabolic physiologic state, as contrasted to the hypermetabolic physiologic state (brought about by the "flight or fight" syndrome, for example). They suggest that it is worthwhile to investigate the possibilities of using TM for clinical application.

15. R. K. Wallace, H. Benson and A. F. Wilson. A wakeful hypometabolic physiologic state. Am. J. Physiol. 221, 795-799 (1971).

"Mental states can markedly alter physiologic function. Hypermetabolic physiologic states, with increased oxygen consumption, accompany anticipated stressful situations. Hypometabolic physiologic changes, other than those occurring during sleep and hibernation, are more difficult to produce. The present investigation describes hypometabolic and other physiologic correlates of a specific technique of meditation known as 'transcendental meditation.' Thirty-six subjects were studied, each serving as his own control. During meditation, the respiratory changes consisted of decreased O_2 consumption, CO_2 elimination, respiratory rate, and minute ventilation with no change in respiratory quotient. Arterial blood pH and base excess decreased slightly; interestingly, blood lactate also decreased. Skin resistance markedly increased, while systolic, diastolic, and mean arterial blood pressure, arterial pO_2 and pCO_2, and rectal temperature remained unchanged. The electroencephalogram showed an increase in intensity of slow alpha waves and occasional theta-wave activity. The physiologic changes during meditation differ from those during sleep, hypnosis, autosuggestion, and characterize a wakeful hypometabolic physiologic state." (Authors' abstract.)

16. R. K. Wallace, H. Benson, A. F. Wilson and M. D. Garret. Decreased blood lactate during Transcendental Meditation. Proc. Fed. Am. Soc. Exp. Biol. <u>30</u>, 376 (1971)(Abstracts).

Eight subjects were investigated in this study. Blood samples were taken from a catheter in the brachial artery every 10 minutes during the following periods: 20-30 minutes before, 30 minutes during, and 10-20 minutes after the practice of TM. Blood lactate concentrations were measured by enzymatic assay. During TM, mean blood lactate levels decreased from an average premeditation value of 11.4 ± 4.1 (SD) mg% to 8.0 ± 2.6 mg% ($p < .005$). After TM, lactates remained low (7.3 ± 2.0 mg%). Increased skeletal muscle blood flow with increased aerobic metabolism during TM would account for lowered lactate levels. Since infusion of lactate ion produces symptoms of anxiety (Pitts and McClure, New Engl. J. Med. <u>277</u>, 1329, 1967), subjective feelings of wakeful tranquility during and after TM may result, at least in part, from the decreased lactate levels. Increased skeletal muscle blood flow may also explain the subjective feelings of muscular relaxation akin to those following exercise. (Adapted from authors' summary.)

17. A. F. Wilson and R. Honsberger. The effects of Transcendental Meditation upon bronchial asthma. Clinical Res. <u>22</u>(2), 278 (1973).

"Twenty-two asthmatic patients who had neither experience with Transcendental Meditation (TM) nor obvious psychological problems were studied. Half of the patients practiced TM for 3 months while the other half read related material daily but did not meditate. Daily symptom and medication information was kept in diaries. Pulmonary function data was obtained at 0, 3 and 6 months and both patients and their physicians were asked to compare the two periods.

"Seventy-nine percent of the patients apparently effectively meditated as evaluated by galvanic skin resistance response. In comparison to control values 94% of the patients had improved airway resistance following TM. There were no large changes in medication used but severity of symptoms was reduced in the TM group. The personal physicians of the patients thought that 55% of these patients were better during TM and 27% worse. However, 74% of the patients reported that TM had benefitted their asthma, 69% thought that it had helped their general health while 63% reported that it had assisted their emotional life. No patient reported worsening of any of these parameters because of TM. Only 11% of the patients thought that reading had any beneficial effect on their general health and asthma. Six months after the study had finished 80% of the patients were still meditating but only 60% thought it was still helping their asthma. Therefore, it would appear that TM is a beneficial adjunct in the treatment of asthma and deserves further definition." (Authors' abstract.)

B. Unpublished Research Papers

1. **A.I.** Abrams. Paired associate learning and recall--a pilot study comparing Transcendental Meditators with non-meditators. Unpublished progress report, Department of Education, University of California, Berkeley, February 1972. (Available from the author.)

In a pilot study of learning and retention of paired associates, Abrams used 30 University of California undergraduates with either no meditation experience (13 subjects), six months' experience in TM (11 subjects), or less than one month's TM experience (6 subjects).

The results suggest that meditators tended to learn quicker and perform better on paired-associates lists than nonmeditators or beginning meditators did. Differences appeared to be directly proportional to list difficulty. There appeared to be no significant linear trend between amount of TM experience and speed of acquisition of the paired associates. Tests of recall revealed significant differences ($p \leq .05$) in both short-term (20 minutes) and long-term (1 week) recall. (Adapted from the author's abstract.)

2. T. D. Anderson. Attitude change as a function of Transcendental Meditation. Unpublished master's thesis, 1973, California State University, Chico, California.

"This research investigates the claims that Transcendental Meditation (TM) produces positive attitude changes over time, and that TMs rely less on external supports for their sources of satisfaction than non-TMs. Four groups were administered an Attitude Questionnaire (AQ) Pre and Post the Queen's (1972) 30 day TM course: Group I = 49 (Pre) and 17 (Post); Group II = 66 (Pre) and 50 (Post) Queen's TM course Ss; Group III = 31 (Pre) and 0 (Post) TM Ss in Toronto who were not at

Queen's TM course; and Group IV = 57 (Pre) and 47 (Post) non-TM Ss. Comparison of Groups' scores indicate: (a) no significant changes occurred in positivity of attitude or external support factors; (b) TM groups revealed significantly greater positivity of attitude $(p < .01)$ and significantly less importance $(p < .01)$ was placed on external support factors than non-TM group; (c) there was no significant correlation between number of hours of TM in an S's life-time and positivity of attitude; (d) and the variables of age and sex had no significant effect. The E concludes that TMs responded in a more positive manner to the AQ than non-TMs, that TMs report less dependence on external factors for sources of support or satisfaction, and that TM may not be the sole factor determining these results. Further research is suggested." (Author's abstract.)

3. D. Ballou. Transcendental Meditation Research: Minnesota State Prison. Research Report, Stillwater State Prison, Stillwater, Minnesota, February 1973.

"The State Trait Anxiety Inventory (Spielberger), a measure of momentary and general anxiety, was administered weekly over a ten-week period to experimental and control groups at the Stillwater State Prison. The first administration of the Inventory was during the week of September 24, 1972. Control group members were sorted into two categories: those who desired to begin Transcendental Meditation and those who were uninterested in receiving instruction. After the second questionnaire administration (two weeks), the experimental group was trained in Transcendental Meditation.

"Preliminary results of this experiment indicate that:

1) Initially, there is no significant difference in anxiety levels between those who want to be instructed in TM and those who were not interested in learning the practice.

2) Within a few days of practice, the meditating group shows significantly reduced levels of both momentary and general anxiety below those of the control groups.

3) Anxiety in the meditators does not show a gradual decline, but is reduced quickly and remains at a low level."

(Author's abstract.)

4. K. Blasdell. The effect of Transcendental Meditation on a perceptual motor task. Submitted in partial fulfillment of the requirements for the M.S. degree, Department of Kinesiology, University of California at Los Angeles, California, December 1971.

It was hypothesized that practitioners of TM will perform better than nonmeditators on a perceptual motor test of speed and accuracy, specifically, the Mirror Star-Tracing Task. College-age subjects (15) meditators and 16 nonmeditators) were chosen randomly. Nonmeditators were tested a few days prior to initiation into the practice of TM. Follow-up measurements after nine months were planned. The subjects sat in a dimly lit room for 20 minutes. The nonmeditators sat with eyes closed and were instructed to relax; the meditators were asked to meditate. Afterwards they performed the Mirror Star-Tracing Task. Each subject was given five trials (one minute apart) in which he attempted to trace between the double lines (1/8th inch apart) forming the star while only being allowed to look at the star's reflection in a mirror placed vertically behind the star, which was flat on the desk. Speed and accuracy were scored.

In general, meditators as a group made "prettier" pictures, took less time to complete the task, and said that they were less frustrated while they were drawing than did the nonmeditating group. The author suggested "...that meditators are more field-independent, relying on their kinesthetic cues rather than being dependent upon the visual field. This would result in their greater ability to resolve the visual motor conflict quickly and without getting bogged down with abstract thinking about what to do." Replication of these results will be attempted in nine months with those subjects who served as nonmeditation controls in the initial experiment.

The conclusion reached was that "...evidence at this point supports the hypothesis that people practicing the technique of Transcendental Meditation will perform more efficiently on a perceptual motor task than those who do not. The results are inconclusive, however, as they have been evaluated subjectively and are susceptible to experimenter's bias."

5. E. Boese and K. Berger. In search of a fourth state of consciousness: psychological and physiological correlates of meditation. Paper submitted for publication, 1972. Pennsylvania State University Medical School, Hershey, Pa.

One week before instruction in TM, 15 subjects (9 males, 6 females; 18 to 36 years of age) were tested with five pictures of the Thematic Apperception Test and the Mooney Problem Check List. Heart rate, breathing rate and amplitude, and GSR were also measured. Subjects were asked to complete a questionnaire that was constructed using the semantic differential technique. The same testing routine was repeated six weeks after all subjects were instructed in TM.

Two subjects dropped out of the study. The results showed that in most tests, there were significant changes after six weeks of practicing TM. A significant decrease was noted in verbalized hostility and anxiety. Physiological data were not analyzed because a number of subjects were thought to be meditating in the initial eyes-closed (i.e., premeditation) period of the second testing session and comparisons were presumably difficult. However, the observed physiological changes tended to agree with those of Wallace: a "marked" decrease in breath rate and depth, a decrease in heart rate, and an increase in GSR during meditation. During the six-week period, meditators missed from 0 to 19 meditations. (Adapted from authors' abstract.)

6. F. M. Brown, W. S. Stuart and J. T. Blodgett. EEG kappa rhythms during Transcendental Meditation and possible perceptual threshold changes following. Presented to Kentucky Academy of Science, Richmond, Kentucky, November 13, 1971 (revised 1972).

This study was conducted to determine whether more efficient functioning results from practicing TM. Performance on certain perceptual tasks was measured before and after TM. The tasks were (a) visual brightness discrimination; (b) simple and (c) complex visual reaction times. Heart and respiratory rates and frontal EEG alpha waves (8-12 Hz, called kappa waves when in the frontal region) were also measured to define the presence of the "meditative state." The meditative state was defined by a decrease in heart rate, an increase in skin resistance, and the presence of EEG kappa rhythms. Female subjects 18-22 years old, 11 meditators (meditating from a few weeks to a few months) and 11 controls, were studied.

Only three of the 11 meditators qualified as actual or criterion meditators when the three physiological measurements were the criterion of the meditative state. For those three individuals, performance on all perceptual tasks improved after meditation. Two of these criterion-meditators had been practicing TM for two weeks and the other, for three months at the time of the tests. Of the 11 nonmeditator controls, one fulfilled the physiological criterion of the TM state. The performance of all the controls worsened.

Ten of the 11 meditators showed the definite presence of the frontal-cortical 8-12 Hz waves throughout most of the 15-minute meditation period. In contrast, three of the 11 nonmeditators showed this rhythm, but with "less consistency" and at a much lower frequency of occurrence. The difference was statistically significant ($p < .01$).

7. R. W. Collier. The effect of Transcendental Meditation upon University academic attainment. Unpublished manuscript, April 1973, University of Hawaii, Honolulu, Hawaii.

"A study was conducted at the University of Hawaii to investigate possible effects of Transcendental Meditation on academic attainment. Subjects for the study were selected from the student body on the basis of an uninterrupted academic record of a semester or more at the University of Hawaii preceding and following the beginning of the practice of Transcendental Meditation. With the help of the Honolulu Center of the Students' International Meditation Society, twenty-nine University of Hawaii student meditators were located. Of these, seven were found to meet the above-stated criterion, and were used in the analysis. The control group for the study is represented by past student bodies of the University of Hawaii. Historical experience indicates that with the omission of the first semester's work the average of students' grades remains essentially level throughout the academic experience. Academic attainment is measured in this study by the use of cumulative grade point ratio (GPR). This ratio is developed on the basis of four points for a grade of A, three for a B, two for a C, etc. This study is historical, that is, the study was started after the data were complete. Students' performances, therefore, were not affected by the study.

"The data indicate a leveling of the GPR for the second semester and a continuation of the rise of the average curve for the third semester following the start of meditation." (Adapted from author's abstract.)

8. P. W. Corey. Airway conductance and oxygen consumption changes in human subjects via a wakeful hypometabolic technique. Unpublished manuscript, 1973, National Jewish Hospital, Denver, Colorado.

Seven transcendental meditators (mean age 31 years, range 23-43; 4 females, 3 males; meditating an average of 25.7 months) and 7 subjects (mean age 32.8 years, range 22-63; 5 females and 2 males), ignorant of the technique, were studied by a series of physiological tests such as large airway resistance, thoracic gas volume (VCO_2 and VO_2) and heart rate. The subjects performed a series of panting exercises during the measurement periods.

Heart rate decreased significantly and specific airway conductance increased significantly after the practice of meditation. The control group, asked to relax, showed no significant changes. Oxygen consumption in seasoned meditators showed significant decreases (15.7%) during meditation.

9. M. Cunningham and W. Koch. Transcendental Meditation: a pilot project at the Federal Correctional Institution at Lompoc, California. Unpublished manuscript, Fall 1973, Federal Correctional Institution, Lompoc, California 93436.

This pilot study was designed to determine whether TM reduces anxiety in prison inmates. Forty-eight inmates from the Peer Counseling Program volunteered; 38 of them were taught TM and received follow-up instruction from February through June 1973; the other ten served as controls. The inmates' feelings of anxiety and their self-images were assessed before and during the program, using generally accepted test devices. The tests were administered on the 11th, 15th and 20th weeks of the program.

The results suggest that (a) immediate and lasting reductions of anxiety were obtained in meditators, and (b) there was a high degree of personality change, which appeared to correlate with regularity of meditation and the relative reduction in anxiety. The changes were statistically significant.

10. V. H. Dhanaraj and M. Singh. Effect of yoga relaxation and Transcendental Meditation on metabolic rate. Presented at the first Canadian Congress for Multidisciplinary Study of Sport and Physical Activity, Montreal, Quebec, Canada, October 1973. Faculty of Physical Education, University of Alberta, Edmonton, Alberta, Canada.

The authors investigated the effect of the yogic exercise Savasana (consisting of relaxing in a supine position while maintaining a certain rhythm in breathing and a calm mind) and Transcendental Meditation on O_2 consumption, heart rate (HR), respiratory rate (RR), and respiratory quotient (RQ). A third, control group was also used. The first experimental group (T1) was trained for 12 weeks in Hatha yoga, which included Savasana; the second group (T2) practiced TM; and the third group (T3) participated in the measurements while resting in the supine position.

Comparison of pre- and post-treatment values indicated that O_2 consumption had dropped significantly in each group: T1 by 10.3%, T2 by 15.5%, and T3 by 3.5%. Differences between the groups were statistically significant. HR decreased by 15% in T1, by 9% in T2, and by 6% in T3. In all three groups, the RR decreased moderately and the RQ was constant at nearly 0.85.

11. L. D. Dick. A study of meditation in the service of counseling. Unpublished Ph.D. thesis, 1973, Graduate College, University of Oklahoma, Norman, Oklahoma.

"The purpose of this study was to investigate the effect of the practice of meditation on the university counselee's experience of well-being as revealed in perception of locus of control of reinforcement, time competence, and self-support orientation. Subjects were randomly selected from the regular client population of the University of Oklahoma Counseling Center and randomly assigned to two sample groups; the experimental group (CM, N = 9) was instructed in the Transcendental Meditation (TM) technique, and the control group (CR, N = 9) was instructed to rest 15 minutes morning and evening each day during the treatment period. A second control group (M) was composed of 8 persons from the university community who on their own had started TM within a week of the CM group.

"The general hypothesis stated that CM > M > CR on internal control, living in the present, and self-support. The Adult Nowicki and Strickland Internal-External Locus of Control Scale (ANS-IE) and

the Time Competence (Tc) and Inner Directed (I) scales of the <u>Person-</u>
<u>ality Orientation Inventory</u> (POI) were administered respectively pre-
and post-treatment to assess change in internal control, living in
the present, and increase in self-support. The <u>Study of Values</u> was
also given at pretest. The three groups were found to be essentially
equivalent on the pretest measures.

"No significant changes were found either between pairs of groups or
within groups on the locus of control variable. The CM group, however, did show a significantly more positive change than did the CR
group in time competence ($p < .025$) and inner directedness ($p < .05$).
In addition, the pre to post positive differences for Group CM were
significant at the .005 level for time competence and at the .005
level for inner directedness. The M group also changed significantly
in the direction of inner directedness ($p < .025$). The mean scores
of the three groups were found to fit a straight regression line on
the Tc and I scales, revealing that CM > M > CR on living in the
present and self-support.

"The findings give support to the hypothesis that the practice of
meditation will aid the university counselee in experiencing a sense
of well-being. To the writer's knowledge no studies of the effects
of meditation on persons in counseling have been reported. Replication and variation of the present design are necessary in order to
generalize the above findings." (Author's abstract.)

12. L. C. Doucette. Transcendental Meditation as an anxiety reducing
agent. Unpublished master's thesis, 1971, McMaster University,
Hamilton, Ontario, Canada.

The following abstract appears on p. 101 of "Treatment: A Report of
the Commission of Inquiry into Non-Medical Use of Drugs, 1972,"
Information Canada, 171 Slater Street, Ottawa, Canada.

"An unpublished pilot study by a student at McMaster University who
used objective tests of anxiety and tension to compare performances
of three groups of university students: (1) naive subjects; (2) those
trained in TM; and (3) those allowed to practice 'meditation' but not
the TM technique. The results suggest that TM had a marked influence
in lowering tension and anxiety levels in those students who had been
instructed properly in its practice."

13. M. F. Fagerstrom. A descriptive study of beginning Transcendental
Meditators. Unpublished Master's thesis in Nursing, 1973, University
of Washington, Seattle, Washington.

"Meditation has become a popular practice in contemporary American
life. In an effort to explore the socio-cultural context of meditation in the Seattle area, a descriptive study of beginning

transcendental meditators was done. Data gathered suggested answers for the following questions: (1) Who are the people who voluntarily begin to meditate? (2) What factors are associated with beginning to meditate? (3) What do people want and expect from meditation? Sixty-one people completed a questionnaire with both closed and open-ended questions at group meeting immediately following initiation in Transcendental Meditation.

"Results obtained indicated the most frequent person to begin meditation was 22 years old, white, male, college student. Influence of one's social circle seems important. Information about Transcendental Meditation is likely to come from a friend and most respondents knew other meditators. The specific characteristics of the meditation technique itself or the reported physical and mental benefits of Transcendental Meditation appealed to most people. However, personal growth was expected from meditation practice." (Author's abstract.)

14. P. C. Ferguson and J. Gowan. The influence of Transcendental Meditation on anxiety, depression, aggression, neuroticism and self-actualization. Unpublished M.S. thesis, 1973, School of Education, California State University at Northridge, Northridge, California. Presented to California State Psychological Association Annual Convention, Fresno, California, January 2, 1974.

"The Cattell Anxiety Scale, the Spielberger Anxiety Inventory and the Northridge Developmental Scale, a measure of self-actualization with subscales for aggression, depression and neuroticism, were administered to an experimental group (N = 31) of university students three days prior to their beginning a program of Transcendental Meditation and to a control group (N = 19) of university students matched for age, sex. Six and a half weeks later the three scales were again administered to both groups under conditions similar to the first testing. All subjects were within the norms on two validity scales on the Northridge Developmental Scale on both testings, indicating test results were valid. Meditators showed a significant decrease on the Spielberger Anxiety Inventory, the Cattell Anxiety Scale, depression and neuroticism. Meditators also showed a significant increase in self-actualization. The control group did not indicate any significant change on any of the scales.

"The same three scales were then administered to a third group (N = 16) of long-term meditators (matched for age, sex and educational level) and their scores were compared to the short-term meditators. The long-term meditators (mean length of 43 months of meditating) were found to show significantly lower levels of anxiety on the Spielberger Inventory and on the Cattell Scale and were also found to show significantly lower levels of depression and neuroticism as well as a significantly higher level of self-actualization than the short-term meditators (mean length of six and one-half weeks meditating). (See also J. Humanistic Psychol., 1975, in Press.)

72

"These results indicate increased psychological health with the length of time meditating. A review of the physiological and psychological literature shows that the present study replicates the findings of other investigators. Meditators are found not only to decrease negative personality characteristics, suggesting useful clinical applications, but they also grow in the qualities of self-actualization found in the healthiest, most creative members of society." (From the authors' abstract.)

15. D. R. Frew. Transcendental Meditation and Productivity. Paper presented at the American Institute of Decision Sciences, Midwest Meeting, April 1973. Academy of Management Journal (in press).

To test the hypothesis that practice of TM produces a positive effect on workers, questionnaires were given to 42 regular meditators (mean age, 26; mean length of meditation experience, 11 months) and to their supervisors and co-workers. The questionnaires were designed to investigate the perceptual differences between the meditator himself and those who work with him.

Practicing TM appeared to be positively related to productivity. Meditators reported that they experienced more Job Satisfaction, improved Performance, less desire to change jobs (Turnover), and better Interpersonal Relationships. The self-assessments furnished by meditators were significantly different from those furnished by the control group on all six variables measured and in agreement with those supplied by their co-workers in at least three cases. In two of the three remaining cases, the co-workers agreed that the meditating group had made a favorable change but did not agree with the magnitude of change.

The results support the proposition that productivity gains are an increasing function of structural level: the higher the level, the greater the gain in productivity. Meditators at higher levels reported that their gains in Job Satisfaction and Performance, their reduced Turnover Propensity and improved Interpersonal Relationships were significantly more positive than those of meditators who work at low levels of the organization. Gains in productivity appeared to be related to the type of organizational structure: the more democratic the structure, the greater the gains in productivity. Increases of significant magnitude were found in Interpersonal Relationships with superiors and co-workers. Also, the participants reported that they were less subject to Turnover if they were working in increasingly democratic organizations.

16. J. Graham. The effects of Transcendental Meditation upon auditory thresholds--a pilot study. Paper submitted in partial fulfillment of the requirements for the B.Sc. degree in Experimental Psychology, University of Sussex, England, June 1971.

Frequency and amplitude discrimination thresholds were measured for 10 subjects before and after 20 minutes of TM and before and after reading a book for 20 minutes (the control condition).

There was a greater percentage improvement (i.e., a narrowing of the discrimination threshold) after meditating for 20 minutes than after reading a book for 20 minutes. The mean percent improvement (compared to discrimination before meditation) in amplitude discrimination after 20 minutes of meditation and after 20 minutes of reading a book was +25.4% and -3.2%, respectively, and for the frequency discrimination task was +37.0% and -15.1%, respectively. The differences were statistically significant ($p \leq .05$) for both tasks. These results tend to support the hypothesis that the regular practice of TM may lower perceptual thresholds. (See also Pirot, p. 86.)

17. D. P. Heaton and D. W. Orme-Johnson. Transcendental Meditation and academic achievement. Unpublished manuscript, February 1974, Department of Psychology, Maharishi International University, Goleta, California.

"A retrospective study compared the Grade Point Average (GPA) of 25 Ss who had begun the practice of Transcendental Meditation (TM) during their undergraduate studies to the GPA of 25 Ss who had received their undergraduate degrees before learning TM. The mean GPA for the TM group rose from 2.52 for the three terms before TM to 3.26 for the three terms after learning TM. The change in GPA for the TM group was significantly greater than the change in GPA for the nonmeditating Ss over an equivalent period ($p < .001$). It was also found that grades tended to continue to improve as one continued the practice of TM. Further research was called for to investigate the possibility that TM may improve the achievements of students at all levels of education." (Authors' abstract.)

18. L. A. Hjelle. Transcendental Meditation and psychological health. Unpublished manuscript, December 1972, Department of Psychology, State University College at Brockport, Brockport, New York.

A study was conducted with 15 experienced transcendental meditators (mean length 22 months) and 21 novice meditators (four days prior to beginning the practice of TM). Experienced meditators were significantly less anxious and more internally controlled than beginning meditators. Experienced meditators also scored significantly higher (i.e., more self-actualization) on 7 of the 12 Personal Orientation Inventory subscales. Results are discussed in terms of the psychological health implication of TM and its potential therapeutic applications.

19. I. M. Klemons. Changes of marginal gingivitis in meditators and controls during an interval of 25 days. Unpublished manuscript, 1973, College of Health, Physical Education and Recreation, Pennsylvania State University, University Park, Pennsylvania.

"Not much is known of possible effects of Transcendental Meditation on inflammatory reactions in normal subjects. A very common inflammation in man is easily seen on the margins of the gingiva. In order to determine whether this marginal gingivitis tends to diminish during intensive meditation, the present study was undertaken.

"A control series of 26 undergraduates at the Pennsylvania State University were given two clinical examinations of the gingiva 25 days apart. No advice on flossing, tooth brushing or other measures of plaque control was given, and all oral examinations were performed by the author. The gingival conditions of these subjects were observed in the middle of an academic quarter, so that anxiety due to academic examinations was minimal. The results of this survey are presented in the upper half of Table I.

"An experimental group of meditators in a residence course at Queen's University, Kingston, Ontario was studied with a similar plan of evaluation of the gingiva, and without advice on the control of plaque on the gingival margins of the teeth. This sample of 46 individuals were meditating 4-6 times a day for 20 minutes per meditation, and performing asanas (moderate physical exercises in the yoga tradition) for about 10 minutes prior to each meditation.

Table I

Gingival Condition

	Worse	No Change	Better	
Controls	12	10	4	$X^2 = 28.0$, $p < 0.001$
Meditators	3	9	34	

"The data in Table I indicate that gingival inflammations significantly improved in a majority of the meditators at the residence course. The controls, if anything, showed deterioration of their gingival tissues.

"Accordingly, it appears that under the relatively disciplined hygienic conditions, regular habits of living, and the combination of transcendental meditation and asanas, most subjects experience a marked reduction in inflammations of the gums. Far more research should be undertaken on possible results of meditation on other inflammatory reactions in the body." (Author's abstract.)

20. D. A. Kolb. Improved reaction time following Transcendental Meditation. Unpublished manuscript, October 1973, Department of Psychology, Maharishi International University, Goleta, California.

Reaction time (RT) to a light stimulus directly in front of the subject was measured. Each subject was seated comfortably before the RT device with his forefinger of his dominant hand resting on a spot 8 inches from an "off" button that takes 500 grams of pressure to depress. Each subject was asked to read the instructions and then asked if he was ready. Upon the reply of "yes," the subject was left alone in the room by himself, and testing began. One entire testing session consisted of:

1. A block of 100 trials with the RT device. The mean intertrial interval was 6.5 seconds, but was randomly varied from three to seven seconds.

2. A TM or rest interval.

3. A 5-minute transition period with eyes open.

4. Another block of 100 RT time trials.

The mean RT for the 53 teachers of TM before meditation was 0.414 seconds, whereas the mean after meditation was 0.378 seconds; significance at the .001 level. (From the author's summary.)

21. G. Landrith, III. Transcendental Meditation and self-actualization. Unpublished manuscript, 1972, University of Kansas, Lawrence, Kansas. (Available from SIMS, Los Angeles.)

Landrith administered a modified version of the questionnaire used by Shelly (M. W. Shelly, "Sources of Satisfaction" and "The Counterevolution," in press, 1973) to assess and better understand the perceived behavioral changes and happiness claimed by meditators. He used a group of 160 transcendental meditators and 145 nonmeditators as subjects. The groups were of similar age and background. The author's abstract follows:

"In summary, this study presents evidence to support the position that Transcendental Meditators exhibit characteristics of self-actualized persons: (1) increased autonomy; (2) increased time spent alone; (3) greater freshness of appreciation and richness of emotional reaction; (4) richer interpersonal relationships; and (5) greater happiness. In addition, evidence gathered by Hebb and Leuba points out that those who are closer to their optimum level of arousal (i.e., happier) would process information from their environment more efficiently. Since Transcendental Meditators are happier, a good case could be made supporting their having a superior perception of reality."

22. W. Linden. The relation between the practicing of meditation by school children and their levels of field dependence-independence, test anxiety and reading achievement. Unpublished Ph.D. dissertation, 1972, New York University, New York. In Dissertation Abstracts International 33(4) (1972).

Three groups were formed, chosen at random from a sample of 84 third-grade boys and girls attending a New York public school: 1) one group received instruction in meditation practice (a Zen type of visual meditation); 2) one was an information guidance group concerned with study skills; 3) one group received no special attention outside the classroom. Results showed that children of the first group tended to become more field-independent and less "test-anxious." Other data showed that reading grades of the first group tended to be better than those of the other groups, but the correlation was not significant.

23. J. S. Lukas. Meditation or simulated meditation by non-predisposed volunteers: some short-term physiological effects. Paper presented at the American Psychological Association Convention, Montreal, Canada, August 1973.

Over a three-month period, 14 subjects practiced TM, another seven practiced a form of meditation in which they thought about or repeated an English phrase rather than the mantra used in TM, and another five did not change their life style in any other way but underwent physiological tests on the same schedule as did the other two groups. The subjects practiced their techniques for 20 minutes, twice daily, and maintained daily records regarding the frequency, duration and subjective effect of these different procedures. Various physiological measurements were obtained monthly, beginning two months before the subjects were randomly assigned to one of the three groups.

Comparing the second set of physiological measurements (i.e., data obtained just before the subjects began practicing their particular meditation or relaxation technique) with the set obtained after three months of practice led to the following conclusions:

(1) Three months of practicing TM or a routine rest period had little effect on heart rate or peripheral blood pulse volume.

(2) When compared to practicing routine periods of rest for three months, practicing TM appeared to have little effect on, or possibly reduced, the relative frequency of "unambiguous" parietal alpha rhythm.

(3) There is some evidence suggesting that practice of TM for three months may instill an EEG state similar to that of Sleep Stage 1 during the meditational periods as compared with other periods of rest of relaxation.

24. J. P. Marron. Transcendental Meditation: a clinical evaluation. Unpublished Ph.D. thesis, 1973, University of Colorado, Boulder, Colorado.

"Three studies were attempted. In the first study, 45 members of the Students International Meditation Society were administered the Activation Deactivation Adjective Check List (AD-ACL), the Similes Preference Inventory (SPI), and form X_1 of the State Trait Anxiety Inventory (STAI). Part of this group, selected at random, meditated for periods of 20 and 40 minutes and situational changes were determined in comparison to control Ss, who were also meditators.

"The second study compared 46 TM meditators to norm groups on preference for novelty and also state and trait anxiety. The third study consisted of a structured interview for 20 TM meditators and evaluated attitudes toward meditation, biographical data, and general interests and values.

"The technique of TM was shown to be an effective method of reducing state anxiety and the tense or nervous feeling usually associated with high activation. Experimental meditation groups were also found to have significantly more feelings of calmness and placidness.

"No significant situational differences were observed for the active interoceptive need for variety. However, meditators as a group were significantly higher on preference for novelty when compared to college samples.

"As a group, the interviewed sample appeared to have interests and personological attributes similar to those traits found characteristic of sensory deprivation-tolerant subjects. These included being nonsmokers, low on anxiety and low externally thrill-seeking. The meditators were more likely to prefer culturally feminine, creative interests and to be readers versus TV watchers. Although characterized by an internal cognitive orientation, most Ss were moderately extroverted and accepting of their need for people. In general, the meditators were likely to have rich inner resources and an appreciation of interoceptive, passive, and intuitive qualities usually associated with Eastern philosophical traditions.

"Although most of the meditators could not be described as self-actualized individuals, many appeared to have qualities suggestive of a striving towards integration and transcendence. These included 1) openness to mystic experience though not necessarily religious; 2) resistance to cultural conformity; 3) strong needs for privacy and detachment; 4) democratic character structure; and 5) creativeness and tolerance for ambiguity.

"While some subjects found the organizational culture of TM supportive, most Ss of the interview sample were more inclined toward an individualistic approach to spiritual concerns and were not typically active in any organized groups. For most Ss, the organizational culture of TM was less an influential factor for the continued practice of meditation than an expectation of increasing awareness and the relaxing and reorienting qualities of the technique itself." (From the author's abstract.)

25. D. E. Miskiman. The effect of Transcendental Meditation on secondary organization. Unpublished Ph.D. thesis, 1973, Department of Psychology, Trent University, Peterborough, Ontario, Canada.

"The present study was conducted to investigate enhanced secondary organization claimed to be facilitated by Transcendental Meditation. Secondary organization was defined as the cognitive ability to abstract a quality or property of an event or object and then generalize that quality or property to all appropriate events or objects. A total sample was randomly divided into two main groups: an experimental group which were taught meditation (n = 60) and a control group which were not taught meditation (n = 60). Each of these groups was divided into two subgroups: one that received a random ordered list of words (n = 30) and one that received a clustered ordered list of words (n = 30). Each of these two subgroups was further divided into three smaller groups: one that received a two minute recall delay (n = 10), one that had a four minute delay (n = 10), and one that had a six minute recall delay (n = 10). The total sample was tested before and after the program of meditation or nonmeditation. The Index of Clustering was implemented to measure the secondary organization.

"It was found relative to appropriate controls that: (a) enhanced secondary organization was facilitated significantly by Transcendental Meditation, (b) meditators demonstrated significantly less clustering variability across word lists, (c) enhanced secondary organization demonstrated by meditators was both strong and continuous, and (d) meditators demonstrated a significantly greater performance in an arithmetic filler task. These results were interpreted as: (a) being in agreement with Transcendental Meditation theory, (b) being in agreement with secondary organization theory, and (c) demonstrating a central concept of Transcendental Meditation--an enhanced awareness of cognitive processes. It was further suggested that future research might (a) investigate the limits of this enhanced secondary organization, and (b) investigate the suppression of information rather than the organizational capacity of those who practice transcendental meditation. (Author's abstract.)

26. D. E. Miskiman. The effect of Transcendental Meditation on compensatory paradoxical sleep. Unpublished manuscript, 1973, Department of Psychology, Trent University, Peterborough, Ontario, Canada.

This study tested the hypothesis that sleep-deprived meditators, being more relieved of fatigue purported to be provided by TM, would show less compensatory paradoxical sleep stage relative to controls during subsequent recovery nights. All subjects were unpaid male and female university undergraduates within the age range 18-25 years and in "normal" health. The meditation group, comprising four subjects, were randomly selected from 12 volunteers at a weekly "group meditation" meeting held at Trent University. The nonmeditation group (also four subjects) were randomly selected from 19 volunteers. All meditators had been meditating for at least seven months, while the nonmeditators had not used any type of meditation practices or biofeedback procedures.

Each subject was recorded for five sleeping nights (the first two nights for all subjects were regarded as acclimatization sessions, and consequently were not scored). A sixth night introduced between the third and fourth sleeping nights was a sleep-deprived session that totalled 40 hours. All recording sessions during the night were held at the same time (12:00 midnight to 8:00 a.m.) to control for any possible effects of subjects' circadian rhythms.

After sleep deprivation for 40 hours, an increase of 25.32% in compensatory REM sleep was observed in the nonmeditation group and a 17.11% increase was observed in the meditation group.

27. D. E. Miskiman. The treatment of insomnia by Transcendental Meditation. Unpublished manuscript, 1973, Department of Psychology, University of Alberta, Edmonton, Alberta, Canada.

"Previous attempts to alleviate insomnia by relaxation training, chemotherapy, or behavior modification techniques have met with limited success due to their short-lasting results, methodological complexities, and/or therapeutic complications. The purpose of the present paper is to report upon a technique, namely Transcendental Meditation, that is simple, easy to learn, and one that demonstrates long-lasting therapeutic results for subjectively reported insomnia.

"Each of a total of ten subjects was interviewed before the start of the study so that data could be gathered concerning the history and form of the subject's insomnia.

"For a period of 30 days before training in the technique, the subjects were asked to note in a daily log the time taken to fall asleep. Each subject was then taught transcendental meditation, and continued for another 30 days to report upon the time taken for sleep onset. At intervals of 60, 120, and 240 days from training, the subjects were asked to report again for a ten-day period.

"There was a significant difference ($p < .001$) between the pre-30-day treatment ($\overline{X} = 75.60$ min.) and the post-30-day treatment ($\overline{X} = 15.20$. There was no significant difference tween the three follow-up periods.

"The results of this treatment for insomnia were very clear and dramatic. It may be argued, however, that the self-reporting method was vulnerable to both intentional and unintentional sources of bias. But this argument is more in line with global reports of improvement rather than specific daily logs--the method used in this study.

"As to the success of Transcendental Meditation as a therapeutic technique, future studies will be necessary to specify the factors involved in the treatment. Since this meditation technique has been demonstrated to reduce anxiety, fatigue, nervousness, and stress, the effect appears to be all-encompassing and restorative, rather than specific. But most important, the technique was dramatically successful and was characterized as being: extremely effective; simple to administer; stable over time; did not induce any unfavorable side effects; and progress could be assessed within a few days after treatment." (Author's abstract.)

28. D. W. Orme-Johnson, G. Authur, L. Franklin, J. O'Connell, and T. Zold. Transcendental Meditation and drug abuse counselors. Unpublished manuscript, 1973, Drug and Alcohol Abuse Control and Prevention Center, Fort Bliss, Texas.

"Seven staff members of the Fort Bliss drug abuse program were tested on the MMPI and other tests before beginning the course in Transcendental Meditation and 10 weeks later. They were compared with a similar group of six non-meditating staff members measured at the same time. After 10 weeks, the experimental group (meditators) showed significantly greater decreases in Manifest Anxiety (Taylor) ($p < .05$), Hypochondria ($p < .05$), and Schizophrenia ($p < .02$) than controls. Meditators also showed greater overall reduction in MMPI scales ($p < .01$). Differences in change on other tests (Maslow's Security-Insecurity Inventory, Purpose In Life Test, and Mooney's

Problem Check List) did not reach significance. These results indicate that subjects practicing Transcendental Meditation produce measurable reduction in the psychological symptoms of anxiety, more maturity and more organized thought and behavior." (Authors' abstract.)

29. D. W. Orme-Johnson, J. Kiehlbauch, R. Moore and J. Bristol. Personality and autonomic changes in meditating prisoners. Submitted to The Correctional Psychologist.

"Twelve narcotics addict prisoners from the NARA program at La Tuna Federal Penitentiary were measured on spontaneous GSR, a physiological index of stress, and the Minnesota Multiphasic Personality Inventory (MMPI) before beginning Transcendental Meditation (TM) and two months later. They were compared with a control group of seven prisoners measured at the same time.

"The results of three groups were compared: regular meditators (meditated at least half of the prescribed times)(N = 5), irregular meditators (N = 7), and control subjects (N = 7). The percent decrease on spontaneous GSR was significantly greater for regular meditators than for irregular meditators ($p < .0005$) or control subjects ($p < .05$). The correlation between the number of times meditated in the two-month period and percent decrease in spontaneous GSR was also significant ($r = .74$, N = 12, $p < .01$). On the MMPI, regular meditators decreased significantly more than controls on scale 7 (psychasthenia, $p < .025$) and scale 10 (social introversion, $p < .05$). They decreased more than irregular meditators on scale 7 ($p < .025$).

"There was a significant correlation between the decrease in spontaneous GSR and decrease in scale 7, obsessive-compulsiveness, of $r = .68$ ($p < .025$). A reduction in compulsiveness indicates an increase in behavioral flexibility. Thus we see a very interesting relationship: the more a subject meditated, the more he simultaneously gained in physiological stability and behavioral flexibility, accompanied by increased social outgoingness. This leads us to conclude that meditation provides a very profound physiological and psychological basis for the rehabilitation of prisoners and that regularity of meditation is crucial to its effectiveness." (Authors' abstract.)

30. L. S. Otis. Meditation or simulated meditation by non-predisposed volunteers: some psychological changes. Presented at the American Psychological Association Convention, Montreal, Canada, August 1973.

"Sixty disinterested volunteer employees of Stanford Research Institute were randomly assigned to a transcendental meditation (TM) group (N = 30), an active control (CA) group (N = 15) or a passive control (CP) group (N = 15). All subjects first received a pre-experimental psychological test and 3 months of baseline physiological measurements. The TM subjects were then trained by qualified teachers in the practice of transcendental meditation (i.e., sitting quietly twice daily for 15-20 minutes just before the morning and evening meals and mentally repeating a Sanskrit word, called a mantra). The CA subjects were assigned to one of two conditions. Group CA1 mimicked the TM procedure except that they repeated an English phrase; Group CA2 mimicked the TM procedure except that they were not given a word or phrase to repeat. Group CP was scheduled for periodical physiological tests but subjects in this group did not change their life style in any other way for purposes of this experiment. All groups received periodic post-training physiological and psychological tests.

"The psychological tests were designed for this experiment and consisted of paper and pencil tests which attempted to evaluate changes in self-concept, projected self-concept and dissonance (Otis Descriptive Personality List), and in behavioral and physical problems or complaints (Otis Physical and Behavioral Inventory).

"The results showed that there were no overall differences between TM and pooled control subjects. An item analysis of the Physical and Behavioral Inventory, however, revealed that more TM subjects than controls claimed significantly greater enjoyment of life, restfulness of sleep, happiness, energy level, sexual adjustment, creativity, awareness and less persistent fatigue.

"An analysis of benefits claimed during an interview conducted 3 months post-training indicated that although TM subjects claimed significantly more benefits than CP subjects, they did not differ in this regard from CA subjects. This finding suggests that the procedure of simply resting twice daily (that is, the CA procedure) may account for at least some of the benefits claimed by practitioners of TM.

"About 50% of the subjects (including the controls that were later trained in TM) discontinued TM within 18 months. The data suggest that there may be predisposing personality factors that discriminate between people who stay in TM and those who discontinue its practice; people who continue TM tend to have better integrated personalities than those who drop out. Predisposing factors that operate to produce a self-selected group should be taken into account when data from TM experiments are interpreted--especially when subjects serve as their own controls." (Author's abstract.)

31. L. S. Otis, D. P. Kanellakos, J. S. Lukas and A. Vassiliadis. The psychophysiology of transcendental meditation--a pilot study. Unpublished report, Stanford Research Institute, Menlo Park, California (in preparation).

A pilot study aimed at determining the teachability of TM to a non-predisposed group of subjects and verifying some of the physiological changes reported in the literature. During the first two months, 60 volunteer subjects (employees of the Institute) not particularly predisposed to meditation were given physiological and psychological tests. Such physiological parameters as brain waves, electromyogram, heart rate, respiration rate, skin temperature, and finger plethysmography were monitored in each subject before, during, and after a period of "rest" in a sitting position. The measurements were taken once a month and were continued thereafter on a monthly basis after some of the subjects were instructed in meditation or in the performance of one of three control procedures. After transducers were placed on the subject, measurements were taken during a one-hour session as follows: 10 minutes sitting with eyes open; 10 minutes sitting with eyes closed; 20 minutes sitting and resting or meditating; 10 minutes sitting with the eyes closed; and, finally, 10 minutes sitting with the eyes open. Blood pressure, oral temperature, heart rate, and body weight were also monitored once a month during nonmeditational sessions. The subjects also received periodic psychological tests.

The subjects were randomly divided into two main groups. One group of 30 subjects were taught the technique of TM. The 30 subjects in the other group were subdivided into three control groups of ten subjects each. The members of one (active) control group were asked to sit and relax for 15-20 minutes every morning and evening as the TM group did. The subjects in the second (active) control group followed the same procedure as the first except that each had been given an English phrase to repeat mentally during the rest period. The members of the third (passive) control group simply came in for measurements on approximately the same schedule as the other subjects did, but did not change their life style (for purposes of this experiment) in any other way.

A major goal of the research was to determine whether beneficial effects of TM may occur in people who may not normally gravitate toward such techniques. Preliminary analysis of the results suggests the following tentative conclusions:

(1) Three months of practicing TM or a routine rest period had little effect on heart rate or peripheral blood pulse volume.

(2) When compared to practicing routine periods of rest for three months, practicing TM appeared to have little effect on, or possibly reduced, the relative frequency of "unambiguous" parietal alpha rhythm.

84

(3) There is some evidence suggesting that the practice of TM for three months may instill an EEG state similar to that of Sleep Stage 1 during the meditational periods as compared with other periods of rest or relaxation.

(4) During an interview conducted at 3 months post-training, TM subjects claimed significantly more global benefits than did either active or passive controls, who did not differ from each other. On a test of motivation, however, TM subjects were significantly more motivated to participate in the experiment than either active or passive control subjects. In a paper and pencil test, although TM subjects claimed significantly greater amelioration of specific behavioral and physical complaints than did passive control subjects, they did not differ in this respect from the active control subjects. This finding suggests that the procedure of simply resting twice daily (that is, the active control procedure) may account for some of the benefits claimed by practitioners of TM.

32. K. R. Pelletier. Altered attention deployment in meditation. Unpublished M.A. thesis, 1972, Psychology Clinic, University of California, Berkeley, California. (Presented at Western Psychological Association Meeting, May 1974.)

"Forty unpaid subjects were selected from an audience attending an introductory lecture on Transcendental Meditation (TM). Design used was a pretest-posttest control group design with each subject serving as his own control and a three-month period between pre- and posttest. Subjects were randomly assigned to two groups of twenty meditators and twenty non-meditators. In order to control for an interaction effect of perceptual indices and TM, half of the subjects in the experimental and control groups were then randomly assigned to both pre- and posttest conditions, while half of the subjects in each group engaged in posttest only. Age (18-26) and sex variables were controlled for by assigning an equal number of males and females in each subgroup since these two factors are the only consistent variables noted in perceptual style research.

"Five indices of perceptual style were administered to all pretest subjects in a double-blind procedure according to the following invariate sequence: 1) three autokinetic effect dimensions; 2) rod and frame test; and 3) embedded figures test. After three months, all experimental and control subjects were tested according to the above procedure.

"Meditators demonstrated increased perceptual acuity on all perceptual indices at the .05 level or better: 1) autokinetic latency decreased (0.001); males decreased more than females (0.001); 2) autokinetic line increased (0.001); 3) autokinetic distance increased

(0.05); 4) rod and frame error scores decreased (0.001); and 5) elapsed time for embedded figures test decreased (0.05); males decreased more than females (0.001). No significant pretest effects.

"Transcendental Meditation tends to increase visual, perceptual acuity. This indicates a significant alteration in an autonomic, developmentally invariate process and clarifies several issues in perception and meditation research. Clinical application is possible with ocular disorders." (Author's abstract.)

33. M. Pirot. Transcendental Meditation and perceptual auditory discrimination. Unpublished manuscript, 1973, Department of Psychology, University of Victoria, Victoria, British Columbia, Canada.

"The stimuli were 40 pairs of tones; each paid had one 2,000 milli-second tone (1,000 Hz, 30 dB) and one 2,225 milli-second tone. Ss had to discriminate after TM or relaxation which tone was the longest in each case, for each 40 pairs of tones.

"The design in brief is as follows:

	First Phase	Second Phase
Group I	Meditation (measure)	Meditation (measure)
Group II	Meditation (")	Relaxation (")
Group III	Relaxation (")	Meditation (")
Group IV	Relaxation (")	Relaxation (")

"All possible orders were represented. N = 32, 8/cell. Repeated measures analysis and one all-between analysis were performed.

"Group II and III analysis showed that meditators performed better after meditation than relaxation, despite which order in which they had meditated.

"A between-groups analysis of the first phases of all groups, pooling the meditation phases and the relax phases, was also significant, demonstrating proficiency of meditators over relaxers.

"Repeated measures analysis on Group I (MM) showed no significant difference. A second meditation did not improve performance on this task. Likewise, an analysis on Group IV (RR) showed no significant difference, consequently no practice effects.

"The results indicate that TM meditators have significantly better perceptual auditory discrimination after a period of meditation compared to a period of relaxation.

"Concurrent psychophysiological measures were taken (GSR, EMG, finger-pulse volume, and EKG), but have not been analyzed as yet; they will comprise a separate manuscript." (Author's abstract.)

34. T. J. Routt. "Low normal" resting heart and respiration rates in practitioners of Transcendental Meditation. Unpublished manuscript, 1973, Department of Psychology, Huxley College of Environmental Studies, Western Washington State College, Bellingham, Washington.

"Heart rate, respiration rate, skin resistance, heart rate variability and finger-pulse volume differences were assessed within and between 12 regular practitioners of a mental technique called Transcendental Meditation (TM) and 12 nonmeditating control Ss. Measurements were recorded before, during and after Ss in both groups meditated and relaxed, respectively. Skin resistance increased significantly during meditation within the TM group. Also, the TM group demonstrated significantly lower heart and respiration rates than the control group throughout pretest, test and posttest periods. These results suggest that the regular practice of TM reduces resting levels of sympathetic activity by shifting autonomic balance in the direction of less sympathetic dominance." (Author's abstract.)

35. C. F. Stroebel. Psychophysiological comparison of alpha biofeedback and Transcendental Meditation in normal subjects and psychiatric patients. Paper presented at American Psychological Association Convention, Montreal, Canada, August 1973.

"This study is a psychophysiological comparison of two techniques which reportedly produce a potentially therapeutic, relaxed, tranquil, pleasurable 'alpha state' which is incompatible with a flight or fight response to stress.

"Twenty normal subjects and 50 psychiatric inpatients matched by age, sex and MMPI high two point code, participated in the study with written informed consent and were randomly allocated to receive training in alpha EEG biofeedback or a simple meditation procedure. Each subject was monitored prior to (control), during, and at two-week intervals with the following psychophysiological measurements: Four simultaneous EEG power spectra (frontal, temporal, parietal, and occipital placements to the contralateral ear), percent time that EEG 8-13 CPS alpha activity was 50% above the control-eyes closed level, skin conductance level, EKG, respiration, and frontalis EMG. Behavioral indices included repeated measurement with the MMPI, MHPA, Clyde Mood Scale, Psychophysiological Diary (normals), Automated Nursing Notes (patients), technician rating scale report, and subjective self report.

"Alpha Biofeedback: Ability to achieve discriminative control of alpha EEG independent of the feedback signal was positively correlated with amount of alpha during the eyes-closed control session. Patients generally required more trials with a greater range of variability in achieving criterion levels and seldom reported relaxed, tranquil feelings during the alpha-on condition. Significant

therapeutic improvement during alpha training was noted in patients
with obsessive-compulsive neuroses without active phobias (e.g., "a
sensation of passively letting my feelings come out").

"Meditation: EEG power spectra demonstrated a lowering of the dominant alpha rhythm frequency interspersed with periods of predominant
theta (5-7 cps) and mixed beta activity in most subjects during their
first and subsequent 20-minute meditation sessions. Total EEG alpha
above threshold did not exceed the control eyes-closed condition.
Subjective reports of relaxation correlated positively with the
lowering of the dominant alpha frequency and with the amount of
theta observed in the power spectra during a session. Consistent
skin conductance decreases of 5-30% of baseline were observed in
both the alpha and meditation groups.

"This study suggests that the two techniques are somewhat different
psychophysiologically by (1) EEG power spectra criteria and (2) rate
of acquisition. Comparatively, the alpha subjects experienced much
greater difficulty in transferring their training to environments
outside the laboratory. Both techniques have apparent value in
helping individuals to reorganize the pace of their daily lives.
More experience with the persistence of observed effects will be
required before judging their effectiveness as adjuncts to established psychiatric treatment" (Author's abstract.) [See also
Roche Report: Frontiers of Psychiatry 4(1), 1, 2, 11 (January 1974),
Hoffman-LaRoche, Nutley, New Jersey.]

36. W. van den Berg and B. Mulder. Psychological research on the effects
of Transcendental Meditation on a number of personality variables
using the Nederlandse Personality Inventory. Unpublished manuscript,
1973, University of Groningen, Groningen, The Netherlands.

The influence of TM on a number of personality variables was investigated. The Nederlandse Personality Inventory (NPV) was taken by an
experimental group (N = 34) one day before starting the course on TM.
A control group (N = 17), consisting of people not applying to take
the course, simultaneously filled out the questionnaire. Experimental and control groups did not differ significantly on any of
the 10 scales of the NPV the first time the test was taken.

Nine weeks later, during which the experimental group practiced TM,
the same questionnaire was again taken by both groups. Five of the
ten scales of the NPV showed significant changes in the expected
direction for the meditators as compared with the nonmeditators.

37. A. Vassiliadis. Longitudinal physiological changes of TM practice. Unpublished study, 1973, Stanford Research Institute, Menlo Park, California. Also presented at the American Psychological Association Convention, Montreal, Canada, August 1973.

Physiological data were obtained from a group of 18 subjects once a month for a period of six months. The physiological measurements included an electroencephalogram (frontal and occipital), hand and forehead temperatures, respiratory and heart rates, skin resistance, and rheoencephalography. After the second month, half of the subjects were instructed in TM while the others served as controls. The study was continued and the number of subjects was increased to about 40. Physiological measurements have been taken at 6, 9, and 12 months after TM instruction.

The author concludes that some physiological changes did occur, some of the changes were not in complete agreement with measurements reported by others on "advanced meditators," and the changes although significant ($p < 0.05$) were not of high statistical significance. However, they do provide sufficient evidence to justify further work.

In addition, his study clearly demonstrated the importance of controls and the need to maintain controls over longer periods of time. The changes that were observed were, for the most part, slow to develop. He suggests that longer periods of time should be used in future studies. Some of the results are scattered in this book (pp. 8, 11, 12, 14, 15, 18).

38. R. K. Wallace. Physiological effects of Transcendental Meditation: a proposed fourth state of consciousness. Ph.D. thesis, Physiology Department, University of California at Los Angeles, California, June 1970. (Also published as a monograph by SIMS, 1015 Gayley Avenue, Los Angeles, California 90024.)

This is a report of the first and most extensive investigation yet accomplished of the physiological and biochemical changes accompanying the TM process. Wallace studied 27 male and female subjects who had practiced TM from 0.25 to 108 months; not all of the subjects participated in all of the experiments. The subjects, acting as their own controls, sat quietly with eyes closed before and after a 20-minute TM period.

Cardiac output, or blood flow volume per unit of time (measured in five subjects with catheters in vein and artery), decreased by 25 percent during TM ($p < .005$). Systolic blood pressure decreased slightly (5-10 mm Hg).

Blood lactate (the ionic form of lactic acid in the blood) decreased by about 50 percent (maximum) during TM and stayed at that low value up to the end of the meditation period and for some 20 minutes thereafter. Initially, only two persons were studied; however, data on six more cases from the Boston area were subsequently obtained. Pitts (Ref. 14 in Section VI of Appendix A) has shown that anxiety symptoms can be induced by infusions of lactate.

Heart rate usually decreased during TM by an average of about five beats per minute.

Blood pCO_2/pO_2 in 15 subjects showed no statistically significant change although total O_2 consumption for 20 subjects decreased by 15 to 20 percent ($p < .001$). Arterial pCO_2 in 10 subjects decreased slightly, whereas pO_2 remained almost unchanged during TM. However, the pH of blood decreased by a statistically insignificant amount.

Base excess of blood decreased significantly ($p < .005$) by about 1.5 milliequivalent per liter. Wallace interpreted this result as indicating a mild condition of metabolic acidosis in the ten subjects studied.

39. L. C. Walrath. Psychophysiological studies of Transcendental Meditation. Unpublished manuscript, 1973, Department of Psychology, Eastern Washington State College, Cheney, Washington.

"Subjects: Three groups of 10 each, selected for scores of 10-12 on the Stanford Hypnotic Susceptibility Scale: a) experienced meditators; b) Ss trained in techniques of auto-hypnosis; c) controls.

"Measures: GSR, HR, Respiration, Parietal EEG.

"Preliminary Findings: Reduction in GSR, HR, and Respiration for all Ss from baseline to treatment; effects persisting through a second baseline for meditators; high incidence of alpha during treatment for meditators and auto-hypnotists, and of theta for half the Ss in each of those groups; interaction between initial base level and the kind of treatment for Respiration and number of discrete GSRs; significant treatment effects for HR and basal GSR; no significant differences prior to treatment. Further studies in progress." (Author's summary.)

40. J. Younger, W. Adriance and R. Berger. Sleep during Transcendental Meditation. In Program of 13th Annual Meeting of Association for the Psychophysiological Study of Sleep, San Diego, California, May 1973.

Eight meditators (seven were TM instructors), who had been meditating an average of 35.5 months and reported normal amounts of sleep nightly, were studied during 31 meditations. EEG activity from two monopolar electrodes of central and occipital origin and horizontal electrooculograms were recorded during each session. Each meditation period,

of usual duration for each meditator, was preceded by a ten-minute
eyes-closed nonmeditating control period. The control and meditation records were unpredictably mixed before being scored by a
single, experienced scorer.

Verbal reports by the subjects left little doubt that they experienced normal meditation periods. Whereas during the control periods the subjects exhibited either waking alert or alpha activity,
during meditation they exhibited waking alert, alpha, or sleep
activity. Almost half of the subjects spent two-thirds of the
meditation periods in "clear, physiological" sleep.

The authors concluded "...a substantial amount of sleep does occur
during TM. We are thus unable to support the conclusion of Wallace
et al (1971) that TM represents a 'wakeful hypometabolic physiological state,' and suggest that some of the physiological changes
they report may reflect unrecognized sleep activity."

C. Personal Communications

1. T. Fehr. Psychologically determined characteristic changes of med-
    itators. Private communication, April 1972 (University of Cologne,
    West Germany). (See also Schöpferische Intelligence, No. 16, 1974.)

The effects of TM on 49 teachers of TM living in Germany in August
1971 were studied, using the "Freiburger Personality Inventory"
(FPI). This questionnaire is similar to the Minnesota Multiphasic
Inventory, and its statistical distribution is well established in
the German population. The FPI contains 212 items divided into nine
groups, each group of items comprising a separate index. The indexes
are Nervousness, Aggression, Depression, Irritability, Sociability,
Calmness, Inconsiderateness, Tension, and Openness (a scale to check
for lying). Three additional indexes (Extroversion, Neuroticism, and
Masculinity) were developed using item analysis techniques.

The subjects were divided into two groups. The first group (20 subjects) consisted of those meditating for less than 4 years (mean of
2.75 years); the second group (29 subjects) consisted of those meditating for 4 to 11.2 years (mean of 7.8 years). For each group, a
separate synthetic control group was constructed from weighted mean
scores and weighted standard deviation values of the population
norms, matching the control and meditator groups with respect to
sex and age. The scores of each meditator group were compared to
those of the corresponding synthetic control group by means of F-
and T-tests.

For the first group (meditating a mean of 2.75 years), only two differences were statistically significant: Irritability (.05 level of
confidence) and Inconsiderateness (.001); the meditators had significantly lower mean scores on both indexes than the controls did. The

second group (meditating a mean of 7.8 years) obtained significantly (.001) lower scores than the controls did on Nervousness, Depression, Irritability, Inconsiderateness, Tension, and Neuroticism. Significantly higher scores were obtained by the meditators on Sociability (.02 level), Calmness (.01), and Masculinity (.001).

Most differences between the second group and its corresponding control group were greater than between the first group and its control group. Only the difference on the Inconsiderateness index was about the same.

The results suggest that the changes observed may be related to the practice of TM. It also appears that the longer that meditation is practiced, the greater are the expected differences between meditators and nonmeditators. (Adapted from author's abstract.)

2. B. C. Glueck. The use of Transcendental Meditation with psychiatric patients. Institute of Living, 400 Washington Street, Hartford, Conn 06101 (Nov. 1973).

"This paper presents the findings of a research study currently being conducted at the Institute of Living, Hartford, Connecticut, utilizing Transcendental Meditation (TM) as an adjunct to the hospital's treatment programs with psychiatric inpatients. The research design involves following patients in the study for a period of 16 weeks, utilizing various behavior descriptors currently employed at the hospital, including the daily computerized Nursing Note factor scores, the Minnesota Multiphasic Personality Inventory (MMPI), and the doctors' and nurses' subsets of the Minnesota-Hartford Personality Assay (MHPA). In addition to these behavior descriptors, psychophysiologic data have also been collected, including six EEG leads from the frontal, temporal, parietal and occipital areas on the dominant hemisphere, and the temporal and parietal areas on the opposit hemisphere; galvanic skin conductance; heart rate; respiratory rate; and electrocardiogram.

"Because of the impossibility of doing any sort of blind or double blind study in a technique of this type, the experimental patients are being matched with comparison twins in the general hospital population, matching being done on the basis of sex, age, and by MMPI profiles, using a computer classification technique.

"Results are discussed in terms of a number of criteria, including a global judgment of condition on discharge made by the treating psychiatrist, changes in the factor scores on the various quantified behavior descriptors, such as the MMPI and the MHPA, and a sequential analysis of changes in the various factors calculated from the Nursing Note.

"A brief discussion of some theoretical considerations about the possible impact on the central nervous system of the meditation technique is given, along with some supporting evidence from the EEG studies." (Author's Abstract) [See also, Stroebel p. 87.]

3. F. Holl. Infrared skin temperature measurements during TM. Private communication, February 1971. (Mr. Holl is studying physiology at the Sports Academy, Cologne, Germany.)

Holl's Ph.D. thesis deals with the coordination of muscles due to the practice of TM. To verify some of the measurements of Ritterstaedt and Schenkluhn (see Ref. 3 below), he used an AGA Thermovision camera and took infrared pictures of ten meditating and five nonmeditating subjects. All meditating subjects showed changes in radiated skin temperature in various areas of the body: equivalent to about 0.5 to 1.5^{O}C in throat and forehead areas and about 3.5^{O}C on the arm and top of the hand. Nonmeditating subjects showed less variation in skin temperature.

4. H. Ritterstaedt and H. Schenkluhn. Measuring changes of the skin temperature during the practice of Transcendental Meditation. Unpublished report, private communication, April 1972. (D433 Mülheim/ Ruhr, Eduardstrasse 7, Germany.)

Ritterstaedt and Schenkluhn used a special transistor (a temperature-dependent diode) to measure temperature changes on the surface of the forehead (just above the depression between the eyebrows). Four long-time meditators (6-10 years of practice) were studied, and about 15 independent measurements of each meditator were obtained.

The subjects pressed a switch each time they began meditating. When they were rested (i.e., in the mornings on workdays, and in the mornings or evenings on holidays), the skin temperature increased by about 0.8^{O}C. When they were tired (especially in the evening), there was a decrease in the skin temperature of about 0.2 to 0.7^{O}C. Changes in skin temperature were observed about five minutes after beginning the first meditation period. Changes began as soon as the subject started the technique within the meditation period. The skin temperature curve during TM showed fluctuations (4 to 8 per minute, with an amplitude of 0.01 to 0.02^{O}C.

Ritterstaedt and Schenkluhn plan more extensive measurements using four locations for determining temperature changes. They will also use nonmeditating control subjects and short- and long-time meditators. (Adapted from authors' summary.)

5. R. Shaw and D. Kolb. One-point reaction time involving meditators and non-meditators. Private communication, 1971.

The objective of this study was to test the hypothesis that TM brings about better coordination between "mind and body," as determined by the speed of a person to react to some stimulus (in this case, a light). The subject's preferred arm was resting on a table, with the middle finger resting on a black square 20 cm away from a switch directly in front of him. After several learning trials, the subject was given a single warning before the first stimulus and then had to be vigilant for 99 more trials.

Two groups were tested. One group was composed of nine meditators who had been meditating one month or longer. The nine subjects in the second group were not meditators. One entire testing session consisted of (1) a few learning trials, (2) a block of 100 trials with the reaction-time device, (3) a 20-minute interval in which one group of subjects meditated and the second group rested with eyes closed, and (4) another block of 100 reaction-time trials.

The meditators had shorter reaction times after meditation than did nonmeditators after rest. After meditation, the meditators "seemed brighter in mood" and were more responsive in conversation.

The authors state: "It is therefore seen that by practicing Transcendental Meditation, the senses of the human body are sharpened and the body can react more efficiently to sensory stimulation. The individual is also brighter in mood and wit, and he is more responsive in conversation."

6. A.S.H. Tjoa. Some evidence that the practice of Transcendental Meditation lowers neuroticism and increases intelligence as measured by psychological tests. Private communication, June 1972.

A high school class of 20 subjects was given a neuroticism test and an intelligence test before 14 of them started TM. A year later, the class was given the same two tests.

Based on a questionnaire, an experimental group was formed of the seven most regular meditators. This group (E) was compared with the "control group" (C) of the nonmeditating subjects in the class (6 subjects). The obtained test scores were converted to centile norms that were different for male and female subjects. Hotelling's T^2 statistic showed that the centroid of test-retest difference scores of the E-group (-26.43 and +27.10) for neuroticism and intelligence, respectively, was significantly different from the centroid of the C-group difference scores (+1.83 and +10.00), the value of T^2 being 5.25, which is significant at the 5% level.

The changes in test scores that took place were that the centroid of the E-group changed from 74.43 and 48.60 for neuroticism and intelligence, respectively, to 48.00 and 75.70. The centroid of the C-group changed from 63.83 and 61.70 to 65.67 and 71.70.

As can be seen, the E-group's neuroticism score was somewhat higher in the first test but was lower in the second test than that of the C-group. The intelligence score of the E-group was lower in the first test but was slightly higher than that of the C-group in the second test. Investigations are under way on a much larger scale to test the reliability of these findings. (Adapted from the author's summary.)

D.   Anecdotal and Related Papers

1. Anonymous. TM, Some Results. Students International Meditation Society, 1015 Gayley Avenue, Los Angeles, California, 1969.

Contains short descriptions of the subjective effects of TM by persons (primarily students) who have been practicing TM for various periods of time. In general, these meditators reported increased joy and happiness, increased capacity to work (e.g., less effort for better grades), and better understanding of self and others.

2. M. A. Blair. Meditation in the San Francisco Bay Area: an introductory survey. J. Transpersonal Psychol. 2(1), 61-70 (1970).

Provides an overview of the first course on the Science of Creative Intelligence (theoretical portion of TM) offered at Stanford University, Spring 1970.

3. S. B. Cox. Transcendental Meditation and the criminal justice system.
Kentucky Law J. 60(2) (1971-72).

Cox suggests that courses in TM be given on a voluntary basis to inmates of correctional institutions. He indicates that initial data
suggest that TM releases tension, anxiety and stress; reduces the
use and selling of illegal drugs; and improves physical and mental
health. He feels that these factors tend to make an individual more
fulfilled and therefore less inclined to criminal behavior, and that
if TM courses are successfully administered, the goals of the rehabilitation institutions may be fulfilled.

4. D. P. Kanellakos. Four levels of speech or utterance. Creative
Intelligence 1(2), 15-21 (1971).

Kanellakos attempts to show how the practice of TM gave him a "deeper and more rewarding understanding" of literature, philosophy,
mythology, and religion.

5. D. P. Kanellakos. Transcendental Meditation. In J. White, Ed.,
The Highest State of Consciousness. Anchor Book A835, Doubleday,
Garden City, New York, 1972, pp. 295-302.

Short introductory material on the effects of the TM practice, based
on anecdotal evidence.

6. J. Robbins and D. Fisher. Tranquility Without Pills. Peter H.
Wyden, Inc., 750 Third Avenue, New York, New York 10077, 1972,
142 pages.

This book is subtitled, "All About Transcendental Meditation."
The authors present introductory material to satisfy the curious,
skeptical person who may want to learn more about TM, how it is
done, what is involved, etc. It includes many brief personal
accounts of how TM has touched or changed the lives of the practitioners, and a question and answer section containing 28 frequently asked questions about TM. It also contains a brief
glossary.

7. A. Rubottom. Transcendental meditation. Yale Alumni Magazine,
February 19, 1972.

A nontechnical article chronicling the growth of TM at Yale University: "Over 1000 Yale students and faculty and alumni have joined a
fast-growing national practice that reduces anxiety and dependence
on drugs."

In addition to the general psychophysiological effects of practicing TM on the individual, the article very briefly describes how one goes about learning TM. It finishes with six brief, signed statements by students relating how TM has decreased their anxiety, hostility and depression, increased their ability to understand the world around them and themselves, and curtailed their dependence on drugs.

8. A. E. Rubottom. Transcendental Meditation and its potential uses for schools. Social Education 36(4), 851-857 (December 1972).

An article reviewing literature on Transcendental Meditation and the Science of Creative Intelligence and discussing the need and the potential for its application in education today.

9. D. E. Sykes. Transcendental Meditation as applied to criminal justice reform, drug rehabilitation and society in general. The University of Maryland Law Forum 3(2), 37-53 (Winter 1973).

A comprehensive review of the physiological, psychological and sociological effects of TM, with an emphasis on the rehabilitation of prisoners and society in general. "By releasing stresses which restrict the use of the full mental potential, TM improves the ability to perceive, evaluate, think and act... A man free from stresses naturally generates happiness and harmony in his surroundings... Crime, delinquency and the different patterns of anti-social behavior arise from deep discontent of the mind; they arise from a weak mind and unbalanced emotions." The author suggests that governmental and private institutions be encouraged to study the benefits of TM.

10. C. C. Tart. A psychologist's experiences with Transcendental Meditation. J. Transpersonal Psychol. 3, 135-143 (1971).

"A psychologist who was generally unresponsive (a personal assessment) to psychological techniques for altering consciousness reports on a year's personal experience in practicing Transcendental Meditation. The altered state (bliss consciousness) was never reached, but important psychological changes occurred. Most prominent was the experience of 'incompletely processed' experiences of the past coming to consciousness and thus being 'finished.' Other effects included a loss of response to alcohol and an increased ability to quiet the mind. Several research directions are suggested." (Author's abstract.)

II. Transcendental Meditation and Drug Abuse

1. H. Benson. Yoga for drug abuse. New Engl. J. Med. 281, 1133 (1969).

Twenty practitioners of TM claimed to have stopped the abuse of drugs such as marijuana, barbiturates, LSD, amphetamines, and heroin. All reported that the reason they no longer took these drugs was because drug-induced feelings became extremely distasteful as compared with those experienced during TM.

2. H. Benson and R. K. Wallace. Decreased drug abuse with Transcendental Meditation: A study of 1862 subjects. In Proceedings of Drug Abuse, International Symposium for Physicians, University of Michigan, Ann Arbor, Michigan, November 10-13, 1970. Lea and Febinger, Philadelphia, 1972. Also printed in Congressional Record, Hearings Before the Select Committee on Crime, House of Representatives, 92nd Congress, First Session, June 2, 3, 4, and 23, 1971. Serial No. 92-1, U.S. Government Printing Office, Washington, D.C., 1971.

Questionnaires dealing with the use and selling of nonprescribed drugs as well as the use of alcohol and cigarettes were given to approximately 1950 subjects who had been practicing TM for three months or longer and who were attending month-long teacher training courses. Of these, 1862 (58% male) completed the questionnaires. The age of the subjects ranged from 14 to 78, and approximately 50 percent were between the ages of 19 and 23. Most had attended college and many had college degrees.

Within three months of starting TM, there was a marked decrease in the number of abusers of all categories of drugs (marijuana, LSD, narcotics, amphetamines, tobacco and liquor). As the practice of TM continued, the subjects as a whole progressively decreased their drug use until, after practicing TM for 21 months, most subjects had completely stopped using drugs. For example, in the six-month period before starting TM, about 80% of the subjects used marijuana, and of those, 28% were heavy users (once a day or more). After practicing TM for six months, 37% used marijuana and of those, only 6.8% were heavy users. The decrease in abuse of LSD and narcotics was even more marked. About 20% of the subjects reported selling drugs before starting TM. Of these, about 72% stopped and about 12% decreased drug-selling during the first three months of practice. Of the subjects who had practiced TM for 21 months or longer, about 96% stopped selling drugs. In addition, about 66% of the subjects had either encouraged or condoned drug abuse before starting TM. Over 95% of these subjects discouraged drug use in others after beginning the practice of TM. Most subjects felt that TM was either very or extremely important in influencing their decrease or termination of drug use. The authors state that TM should be investigated as an alternative to drugs. (See also Benson et al., 1974, Appendix D.)

3. E. Bräutigam. The effect of Transcendental Meditation on drug
    abusers. Unpublished report; research conducted at City Hospital,
    Malmö, Sweden, December 1971. (Available from Students' Inter-
    national Meditation Society, Los Angeles, California.)

Describes a study of 20 drug users 17-24 years old, consisting of
a control group of 10 nonmeditators and a group of 10 who became
meditators. The subjects had developed hepatitis, presumably as a
result of drug abuse. Twelve of the subjects had histories of hashish use; the others had used "harder" drugs (LSD, amphetamines and
opiates) more than 10 times in the six months prior to the experiment. The experimental and control groups each consisted of six
hashish and four hard-drug users. During the first three months of
this six-month study, the experimental group was prescribed and
learned meditation (following procedures recommended by SIMS) while
the control group was offered counseling therapy. The control group
was prescribed TM near the beginning of the second three-month period.
Questionnaires were administered at the beginning of the study, at
three months, and at six months.

The average number of times the various drugs were used per month is
shown below.

Group	May		June		July		Aug.		Sept.		Oct.		Nov.	
	(1)*	(2)	(1)	(2)	(1)	(2)	(1)	(2)	(1)	(2)	(1)	(2)	(1)	(2)
E[+]	19.2	2.4	0.6	0.0	1.2	0.4	3.0	0.2	5.2	0.6	6.1	1.3	6.1	0.8
C	20.5	3.0	18.5	4.5	18.4	6.1	18.2	6.8						

*(1) = Hashish; (2) = LSD, amphetamines, opiates.
[+]E = experimental group (learned TM in June); C = control group
  (learned TM in September).

The reported reduction in use of hashish was statistically significant (p < .01). Two of the controls stopped use of drugs spontaneously; one experimental subject never started to meditate regularly
and did not refrain from drugs in any of the six months.

At the end of the six months, six of the ten experimental subjects
could be classed as regular (twice a day) meditators, and these used
hashish three times per month on the average. The four who did not
meditate regularly were using hashish about 10 times per month and
their trend of use was upward.

Five of the controls who started meditating regularly in September
decreased their drug abuse in approximately the same way as the
experimental group did.

No changes in work habits were noticed (one-third of the subjects were out of work for the major part of the time). No changes in leisure habits were noted, but the experimental subjects reported that they had become more active and had more energy to do things in their leisure time. On the self-evaluating questionnaires, the experimental subjects reported improvements in "adjustment" (p < .05), whereas the controls remained unchanged. The experimental subjects felt that they were more relaxed and less tired, had less "anxiety," and were more extroverted; the control subjects developed slightly in the other direction, but the groups did not differ significantly.

Their "general condition" was judged by observing their overt behavior. The experimental subjects improved, compared with the controls, in tension-restlessness (p < .001), psychomotor retardation (p < .10), and flaccidity (p < .05). The author described certain factors that may have influenced the subjects' behavior: (1) the experimental subjects knew of the probable effect of TM on drug abuse; and (2) they were instructed to refrain from drugs for five days prior to TM instruction (nine of ten subjects succeeded, which indicated that they were not physiologically addicted).

4. V. H. Dhanaraj. Influence of Transcendental Meditation and Hatha Yoga on drug abuse. Unpublished Ph.D. thesis, 1973, University of Alberta, Edmonton, Alberta, Canada.

Using questionnaires, practitioners of TM and Hatha Yoga (HY) were surveyed to determine how usage of illegal drugs, alcohol, and tobacco changed after learning and practice of these techniques. The author concluded that "...drug users change their habit considerably as a result of TM and HY practices.

"It appears that a large percentage of the drug users have the desire to give it up, but they are unable to do so, owing to the lack of other interesting activities to substitute drugs. TM and HY seem to offer the type of experiences the drug users need, not only in providing relaxation, but also in changing attitudes."

5. A. A. Gattozzi and G. Luce. Physiological effects of a meditation technique and a suggestion for curbing drug abuse. Mental Health Program Reports--5, National Institute of Mental Health, Department of Health, Education and Welfare Publ. No. (HMS)72-9042, pp. 377-388, 1971.

A review of the work on the physiological effects of TM by Wallace and Benson, including their drug abuse studies. It is primarily a review of Dr. Wallace's Ph.D. thesis.

6. K.-D. Kniffki. Transzendentale Meditation--TM u. a. eine nichte-
chemische Methode gegen Drogenmipbrauch. Niedersachsisches
Arzteblatt <u>44</u>, 805-809 (1971).

A review article in a German medical journal on the physiological
effects of TM and decreased drug abuse as a result of practicing TM.
The article is written by a physicist and is primarily based on the
Allison; Wallace; and Wallace and Benson articles. The author's
abstract in English follows:

"The scientific basis of Transcendental Meditation (TM) is described
and the main fields of application are indicated. Physiological and
biochemical changes during the practice of TM indicate a fourth major
state of consciousness. It is suggested that further research be
done to detect the fourth state of consciousness on the microphysio-
logical level, i.e., on the cellular and molecular level. Further
on it is suggested that this technique be practiced as one possibility of non-verbal education in order to unfold and harmonize the
personality. Research in the USA has shown that TM may help in the
reduction of drug abuse. A proposal is made to use TM in Germany
as a non-chemical therapy for drug addicts and as a preventative
measure in medical applications."

7. B. R. Marzetta, H. Benson and R. K. Wallace. Combatting drug dependency in young people: A new approach. Medical Counterpoint,
pp. 13, 32-36 (September 1972).

"While researching how physiologic adjustments to the stresses of
modern living may contribute to heart disease, the authors found
that many of their young subjects (college students) who practiced
a form of meditation that helped them 'cope' also markedly reduced
their dependency on drugs--marijuana, LSD, amphetamines, barbiturates, even narcotics such as heroin. This self-administered
mental exercise may be of major importance in preventing those well-
placed young people, the potential leaders of our society, from
descending the abyss of addiction, to the dismay of their parents
and family physicians". (Authors' abstract.)

8. L. S. Otis. Changes in drug usage patterns of practitioners of
Transcendental Meditation (TM). Unpublished report, Stanford
Research Institute, Menlo Park, California, January 1972.

A retrospective study of a sample of 620 teacher trainees of TM who
returned questionnaires distributed to approximately 900 subjects
indicated that of over 396 former drug users, a significant proportion completely gave up the use of drugs within 0-20 months of starting TM. Forty-two of 49 users of opiates discontinued their use.

The degree of drug dependence of these subjects and the reliability of their recall, however, are not known. Also, whether they had in fact given up drugs before starting TM or after some period of practice is not known.

9. M. Shafii, R. Lavely and R. Jaffe. Meditation and marijuana. Practice of Transcendental Meditation contributes significantly to discontinuance of marijuana use. Am. J. Psychiatry 131(1), 60-63 (1974).

"In a socio-psychological survey of 126 subjects who have practiced Transcendental Meditation (TM) between 1-39 months and 90 matched control subjects we found:

"1. Ninety-two per cent of the meditators who had practiced TM more than two years decreased significantly their use of marijuana, and 77% totally stopped their usage.

"2. In this group of meditators who had practiced TM more than 2 years, during the first 3-month time period following their initiation to TM, 69% totally stopped their use of marijuana in contrast to the control group's 15% stoppage (p < .01).

"3. In Group I (meditators practicing TM 1-3 months) there was a 46% decrease and a 23% stoppage in the use of marijuana during the first three months following their initiation to TM. In the control group there was a 15% stoppage during the same time period.

"4. In Groups II (meditators practicing TM 4-6 months), III (meditators practicing TM 7-12 months) and IV (meditators practicing TM 13-24 months) there was also a significant decrease and stoppage in the use of marijuana during the first three months following their initiation to TM.

"5. The longer a group had practiced meditation, the more they reported a decrease or discontinuation of marijuana use.

"6. The mean of the frequency of use of marijuana per month for the entire population of meditators before initiation to TM was 7.3. The control group's mean was 3.6. Following initiation to TM, the mean of the meditators as a group dropped to 2.8 whereas the control group's mean stayed the same." (Author's summary.)

10. H. C. Shands. Drugs, religion and psychiatry. New Engl. J. Med. 282, 104-105 (1970).

Shands comments on Benson's letter (Ref. 1, this section) describing the serendipitous finding that TM has a "therapeutic effect upon drug abuse." He mentions that psychiatry cannot exclusively be seen as a medical specialty, treating mental illness by specifically medical methods. Depending on the point of view, the treatment followed will vary: TM, Yoga, Zen, Synanon or Alcoholics Anonymous. Each can be considered a method of treatment. He concludes, "I agree wholeheartedly with Dr. Benson that intensive (especially theoretical) exploration of the implications of transcendental experience for 'mental illness' is indicated."

11. W. T. Winquist. The effect of the regular practice of Transcendental Meditation on students involved in the regular use of hallucinogenic and "hard" drugs. Unpublished manuscript, 1969, Sociology Department, University of California at Los Angeles, Los Angeles, California.

"The first survey via questionnaire dealing with changing drug usage patterns of TM practitioners. About 600 questionnaires were distributed and 484 were returned completed. It was found that 143 were regular users of illegal drugs. Of those who used marijuana regularly, 84 percent stopped, 14.5 percent substantially decreased, and 1.5 percent increased their use of marijuana after at least three months' practice of TM. 111 used hallucinogenic drugs (LSD, mescaline, peyote), and 42 used hard drugs (heroin, morphine, amphetamines, and barbiturates). Of the last two categories, 86 percent stopped and 14 percent reduced their use of hallucinogenic and hard drugs after three months' practice of TM (or more)." (Author's abstract.)

III. Theory of TM and Altered States of Consciousness

1. H. H. Bloomfield, M. Cain, D. T. Jaffe and A. Rubottom. What is Transcendental Meditation? In What is Meditation? J. White, Ed., Doubleday-Anchor, New York, May 1974.

This article is written in clear, simple terms for a mass audience. The history of TM's introduction to the United States is given, along with a brief description of Maharishi's life and the process of TM (using a mantra). The philosophy of TM and the initiation ceremony are explained, and the World Plan is outlined. The remainder of the article presents an overview of TM research in all areas thus far examined by science: psychophysiology, psychology, sociology. The authors suggest that "TM can be conceived as a kind of self-administered psychotherapy" which those concerned with mental health should examine because of its easy accessibility, low cost and consistent results.

The authors have also prepared a book with the title Meditation and Stress (Delacourt, N. Y., 1975).

2. D. N. Day. Meditation: a multistage learning model. Unpublished
    Ph.D. dissertation, 1972, Department of Business Administration,
    University of California, Berkeley, California.

    This dissertation develops a formal (theoretical) model of the
    process of learning meditation "...as described in Patanjali's
    Yoga sutras..." that unifies the structural and teleological
    elements of the process in a way that allows a connection to be
    made between behavior (like concentration) and physiological var-
    iables (like EEG). It also provides a means to quantitatively
    measure the behavior involved in meditating. No experimental
    results are provided.

3. T. de Chardin. The Phenomenon of Man. Harper Torchbook TB383,
    Harper & Row, New York, 1959, 1961.

    The author proposes that mankind in its totality is a phenomenon to
    be studied, described, and analyzed like any other phenomenon; it
    and all its manifestations, including human history and human values,
    are proper objects for scientific study. To accomplish the above,
    de Chardin argues that we must adopt "an evolutionary point of view."
    Phenomena are not static (including the evolution of man), and they
    have both an inner and outer sphere that must be studied simultan-
    eously as they converge to a unity that the author calls Omega.

4. R. Fischer. A cartography of the ecstatic and meditative states.
    Science 174, 897-904 (1971).

    The author presents his map of inner space: a continuum extending
    from perception to hallucination, in which increasing "trophotropic"
    or hypo-arousal leads to meditative states and increasing "ergotropic"
    or hyper-arousal, to hallucinatory experiences.

5. J. Forem. Transcendental Meditation: Maharishi Mahesh Yogi and the
    Science of Creative Intelligence. E. P. Dutton, Inc., 201 Park
    Avenue, New York, New York, 1973.

    This book describes the benefits of TM, the history of the movement
    of TM, the Science of Creative Intelligence, and informative material
    concerning the philosophy, psychology and principles of TM.

6. E. Gelhorn and W. F. Kiely. Mystical states of consciousness:
    neurophysiological and clinical aspects. J. Nerv. Ment. Diseases
    154, 339-405 (1972).

    "The relationship of the trophotropic and ergotropic systems of
    autonomic-somatic integration and their relevance to a variety of

emotional states and levels of consciousness is reviewed. The importance of proprioceptive afferent feedback to the reticular formation and hypothalamus for the maintenance of ergotropic responsivity is indicated together with the beneficial clinical effects of certain behavior therapies which employ skeletal muscular relaxation as a technique for modifying central nervous system arousal. The neurophysiological basis of Asian and Oriental meditation exercises is reviewed as well as the basis of Yoga ecstasy. EEG patterns in states of meditation indicate that conditions reflective of trophotropic dominance are compatible with full awareness. The failure of habituation of alpha-blocking by sensory input would appear to indicate that some ergotropic influence continues to be exerted upon the cerebral cortex in the meditation state and seems in some way to be a correlate of the heightened perceptual sensitivity reported by such subjects. Clinical observations suggest that certain formerly drug-dependent adolescents and young adults have achieved psychological benefit from systematic practice of meditation. Its potential for therapeutic benefit in certain states of anxiety, phobia, and psychosomatic disorder is suggested."
(Authors' abstract.)

7. D. Goleman. Meditation as meta-therapy: Hypotheses toward a proposed fifth state of consciousness. J. Transpersonal Psychol. 3(1), 1-25 (1971).

Goleman is a practicing meditator who spent about a year and a half in India studying humans reportedly in the fifth state of consciousness. He offers 14 testable hypothesis on TM and its effects on anxiety level, need for sleep, personality, musculature, posture and fatigue. Systematic desensitization is compared to meditation. He also discusses the concept of "unstressing," or normalization of the nervous system, and suggests it may serve the same psychological function for the meditator as do dreams.

In a personal communication (August 1971), the author states: "This paper connects my experience as both a clinical psychologist and a meditator. I call meditation a 'meta-therapy' because it accomplishes as side effects what psychotherapy takes as its major goals, and can establish the meditator in a new state of consciousness (discontinuous with our normal state) where the 'fourth state,' pure awareness, is fused with the waking, sleeping, and dreaming states. I ground discussion of this 'fifth state of consciousness' in current psychological theory. I delineate the processes by which the fifth state is reached through meditation, and analyze the structure and function of these processes in terms of behavior therapy, Reichian variations on psychoanalysis, and in light of physiological studies. Attributes of the fifth state are enumerated and related to Maslow's Theory Z. From the body of the paper are generated fourteen testable hypotheses about the fifth state and the processes for attaining it through meditation."

8. J. Grant. Meditation: means & ends--a conversation with Demetri Kanellakos. In J. Grant, Ed., The Geocentric Experience. Lamplighters Roadway Press, 44 Fairview Plaza, Los Gatos, California, 1972.

    Introductory material on the theory, mechanics, and practice of TM and the growth of consciousness.

9. D. P. Kanellakos and W. Bellin. The practice of meditation as a means to the fulfillment of the ideals of humanistic and transpersonal psychology. Presented at the 10th Annual Meeting of the Association for Humanistic Psychology, Honolulu, Hawaii and Squaw Valley, California, 1972.

"For thousands of years people throughout the world from many different cultures and civilizations have practiced meditation in one form or another. Though interest in meditation has not been widespread in Western civilization during recent centuries, the years through the 60's and 70's have witnessed a very significant awakening of such interest. Unfortunately, there is at present much confusion about the nature and the purpose of the practice of meditation. One major confusion is that meditation is often viewed as an end in itself rather than a means to an end. A second major confusion is that the results of meditation, both during its practice and after its practice during daily activity, have often been confused with the practice itself. The result of the first confusion is that people orient their whole life around the meditative practice and become reclusive, losing all interest in outward experiences and activities. The second confusion results in people trying to produce the meditative state (1) by force (controlling breathing, concentrating against thoughts, etc.) or (2) by auto-suggestive techniques (e.g., suggesting to oneself, 'I am becoming relaxed.'). For some who meditate, or try to, it also results in the attempt (in daily activity) to copy the habits, life styles, dispositions, etc., of many who do meditate successfully. Since such practices are unnatural, quite difficult, and usually not very effective, most people find that they cannot or do not continue for very long, and the myth grows that meditation is only for the chosen few who can take the rigor, discipline, and austerities. We are fortunate that recently there has been a revival of understanding in meditation as a means to an end and of the total simplicity, naturalness, and easiness of its practice. Transcendental Meditation (hereafter referred to as TM), as taught by Maharishi Mahesh Yogi, is a simple, natural technique of meditation that can be practiced by anyone. It does not involve any effort, concentration, or control of the mind or body, or any special posture. It does not involve any suggestion or auto-suggestion and it is not time-consuming (one meditates twice per day for 15 minutes each time). It does not require any change in life style, dress, or diet; and if such changes do take place, they are the natural and spontaneous

result of the growth of the individual through meditation. Changes
of this kind frequently do occur, because the mental process during
TM brings about a psychophysiologic shift (i.e., a new style of
functioning of the nervous system), which can be empirically verified and scientifically studied.

"The purpose of TM is the progressive expansion of human consciousness (awareness) and an integrated enhancement of all aspects of
daily life as an automatic and spontaneous consequence of that expanded consciousness. Consciousness is defined as the capacity to
be aware, to know. Human beings are usually found to possess the
capacity for two kinds of awareness: (1) awareness, through the
five sense modalities, of the outer, objective environment, and
(2) awareness of the inner subjective environment (e.g., awareness
of thoughts and emotions). In the practice of TM one very easily
achieves a third kind of awareness, a unique psychophysiological
state defined phenomenologically as transcendental consciousness
(i.e., awareness of pure, undifferentiated consciousness, devoid
of any object). This condition has been defined as a wakeful,
physiologic hypometabolic state. The existence of this third kind
of awareness (transcendental consciousness, or TC) can be experientially verified by anyone who undertakes instruction in TM, and
the physiological correlates to that state of consciousness are
well documented.

"Practitioners of TM report that the automatic result of experiencing
TC is that after long meditation and while engaged in daily activity,
all other forms of awareness (both inner and outer) are increased
in their richness, intensity, positivity, and vitality. This enhanced awareness manifests behaviorally in increased creativity,
power, synergy, spontaneity, stability, richness, and harmony in
interpersonal relations, and in a gradual adoption of what Abraham
Maslow has called B-values. It manifests psychologically in better
health, more energy, and a sense of physical well-being. The regular daily practice of TM results in a gradual increase in the
capacity for awareness both in and out of meditation. This continues over a period of some years until, finally, TC is permanent-
ly and spontaneously maintained at the same time as all other forms
of awareness. This permanent state of consciousness, which is the
goal of meditation, is called cosmic consciousness in the Vedic
philosophical tradition of India. It is a 'higher' state of consciousness if we define 'higher state of consciousness' as a heightened capacity for awareness. This cumulative effect, on human life,
of the regular daily practice of TM can be personally verified by
anyone and can also be (and is being) studied (1) experientially
and behaviorally by the methods of empirical psychology, and (2)
physiologically by the methods of the science of human physiology.
Thus, we propose that the practice of meditation may be a means to
the fulfillment of the ideals of Humanistic and Transpersonal
Psychology." (Authors' summary.)

10. Maharishi Mahesh Yogi. The Science of Being and the Art of Living. International SRM Publications, new revised edition, 1966. (Available at any SIMS center. Also published as a Signet paperback, new edition, 1972.)

The basic textbook on the theory and method of reaching transcendental consciousness. It describes the experience of self-knowledge and reaching one's full potential. One cannot learn the technique of TM from this book alone; personal instruction is required.

11. Maharishi Mahesh Yogi. Commentary on the Bhagavad-Gita. International SRM Publication, 1967, Chapters 1-6. (Also available in paperback: Book 2913, Penguin Books, Baltimore, Maryland, 1969.)

Describes the principles of "skill in action," the experience of transcending as a technique of "realization of the self" and the "development of the full potential of the self." Describes the relationship of the self to the actions of the self and to the rest of the cosmos.

12. A. H. Maslow. Toward a Psychology of Being. D. Van Nostrand Co., Inc., Princeton, N. J., 2nd ed., 1968.

An excellent description, in western psychological terms, of the person who is well advanced toward self-actualization, i.e., realizing his full potential. The description of the "peak" experiences, or what happens as one evolves toward his full potential. Maslow states that only one person in a few hundred reaches his full potential.

13. Orme-Johnson, D. W., "Meditation as Psychotherapy," Department of Psychology, Maharishi International University, Los Angeles, CA 1972.

This paper reviews evidence that the practice of TM is an effective agent in reducing tension, eliminating accumulated stresses, and bringing a person into a healthier, more responsive interaction with others and his environment.

14. Proceedings of the First International Symposium on the Science of Creative Intelligence, July 18 to August 1, 1971, University of Massachusetts, Amherst, Massachusetts and Humboldt State College, Arcata, California, August 14-18, 1971. (Available from SIMS, Los Angeles.)

Creative intelligence is defined by Maharishi Mahesh Yogi as the impelling life force that manifests itself in the evolutionary process through creation of new forms and new relationships in the universe. The science of creative intelligence is a systematic study of its nature, origin and development, and incorporates a natural means (i.e., TM) of experiencing its whole range. The science of creative intelligence presumably draws together the source and goal of all knowledge, thus bringing to light one common basis and interrelationship among all disciplines. It was the purpose of the 1971 International Symposium to exemplify and examine the interdisciplinary value of the science of creative intelligence through the contributions of participants from various fields.

15. G. E. Schwartz. Pros and cons of meditation: current findings on physiology and anxiety, self-control, drug abuse, and creativity. Presented at the American Psychological Association Convention, Montreal, Canada, August 1973. (See also Schwartz, Appendix D, p. 140.)

After a review of eight studies by others and nine studies conducted by Schwartz and his colleagues, Schwartz concluded by stating:

"Based on this set of findings, the question arises whether it is possible to say anything about the pros or cons of meditation training at this time. Our general conclusion is that meditation practices, if utilized regularly and in moderation, can have some beneficial psychological and physiological consequences for a person, particularly in this overstressed culture. There may well be an evolutionary precedent for meditative practices, since scrutiny of primitive human societies and even societies of lower primates suggests that typically an hour a day is spent in quiet sitting in what appears to be 'self-reflective' behavior. However, in the same way that too much activity and stress can have deleterious effects on physiological and cognitive functioning, it follows that too much meditation, like the effects of long-term sensory deprivation, can have deleterious consequences as well. It is well known that the nervous system needs sufficient intensity and variety of external stimulation to maintain proper functioning, and there is no evolutionary, ethological or biological precedent to justify massive and prolonged (on the order of eight hours a day) self-induced meditative practices. Based on an extensive review of the Zen meditation literature, the theory of meditation as a hypoxic state proposed by Watanabe, Shapiro and Schwartz (1972) illustrates the potential physiological consequences of prolonged meditative practices continued for many years. Clearly, systematic research is needed to uncover the mechanisms of meditation and the conditions under which beneficial effects can be obtained."

16. C. C. Tart. Scientific foundations for the study of altered states of consciousness. J. Transpersonal Psychol. $\underline{3}$(2), 93-133 (1971). See also Science $\underline{176}$, 1203-1210 (1972) for another version.

Tart proposes an expansion of science, now limited to "finite-state science," to include "state-specific sciences." These sciences would examine altered states of consciousness and would be referred to as the "Science of Meditation," "Science of Hypnosis," "Science of ESP," etc. He calls for the development of new methodologies and new approaches. Among the new criteria for acceptance of a method may be such matters as what the experimenter would have to know or to have experienced in order to be able to carry on the necessary experiments or to discuss them.

17. K. Vanselow. Meditative exercises to eliminate the effects of stress. Hippokrates (Stuttgart) 39, 462-465 (1968).

Vanselow compared the effects of TM with those of autogenic training, suggestive therapy, and psychoanalysis. He believes that TM is quite different from psychoanalysis: "The latter considers the blocked experiences and strengthens the mind by decomposing the blockages. Transcendental meditation strengthens the thought areas which are freely accessible to the conscious mind and thus the blocked experiences become meaningless." He continues, "You can either root out the complexes one by one like weeds or you can make the inner mental soil so healthy that complexes don't grow in it any longer."

IV. The Psychobiology of Other Meditation Techniques

1. Y. Akishige. A historical survey of the psychological studies in Zen. Kyushu Psychol. Stud. 5, Bull. Fac. Lit. Kyushu Univ. 11, 1-56 (1968).

In Japan, several universities have Zen Institutes, where the scientific study of the physiology, psychology, and medical aspects of the practice of various forms of Zen meditation is carried out.

This bulletin contains a 56-page historical survey of such studies done at various institutions, spanning the period from about 1920 to 1968. Eight other papers on various subjects are also included; the work described in these eight papers was done at Kyushu University. The survey paper includes the physiological changes reported by Onda (Ref. 9, this section) plus some electromyographic studies. Akishige also reports that "the blood pH of two Zen monks who practiced Zasen was significantly reduced, by 0.03 and 0.04 units, whereas among the control group little change was reported. Judging from the simultaneous decrease of sodium bicarbonate in blood plasma, this decrease of pH may be due to the control of the respiratory center through Zasen."

Zen monks were also examined psychologically. They showed nearly average results in Rorschach tests, exhibited normal scores in a self-consciousness test, and showed no differences between the self-estimated ideal and the actual self. Motives of practitioners of

Zen have also been extensively examined. Zen and hypnosis are compared in this article. Finally, the creative process and Zen are evaluated and briefly reported. On page 51 it is mentioned that, "...as pointed out by Meada and Honda in the article 'Zen Buddhism and Psychoanalysis,' Jap. J. Hypnosis, Vol. 9, pp 9-13 (1964), the way Zen takes to attain enlightenment through a specific bodily set is a very severe way that is not for everyone."

2. B. K. Anand, G. S. China and B. Singh. Some aspects of electroencephalographic studies in Yogis. Electroencephalog. Clin. Neurophysiol. 13, 452-456 (1961).

The authors report on electroencephalographic studies of four yogis practicing Raj Yoga and, presumably, during samadhi. All yogis showed prominent alpha activity in their normal resting records. During samadhi, all had persistent alpha activity with well-marked increased amplitudes. External stimuli (like strong light, loud banging noise, touching with hot glass tube and tuning fork) blocked resting alpha rhythm and changed it to a low-amplitude, high-frequency wave when the yogis were not meditating. This blocking action did not show any adaptation to repetition of the same stimuli. None of these stimuli produced any blockage of the alpha rhythm when the yogis were in meditation (samadhi). No changes in alpha activity appeared when the yogis (during samadhi) were exposed to pain such as immersing hand in ice water.

3. B. K. Bagchi and M. A. Wenger. Electro-physiological correlates of some Yogi exercises. Electroencephalog. Clin. Neurophysiol., Suppl. 7, 132-149 (1957).

Various physiological processes were monitored in 45 subjects during various yogic practices in 98 sessions. Electroencephalogram, electrocardiogram, electromyogram, plethysmogram, respiration, electrical skin resistance, skin temperature, and blood pressure were recorded during different yogic postures accompanied by meditation. Heart rate decreased 6-9%, but never went below 62 per minute during meditation. Respiration rates of 12 subjects in 9 of 16 sessions never went higher than the rate during the control period. Respiration rate decreased an average of 23%, but it dropped by 50-60% in some cases at some times. At times, respiration became so shallow that it was uncountable. Electrical resistance (GSR) of the palm always increased; the median increase was 56%, with a high of 106%. Blood pressure rose minimally in some subjects, but dropped 20 mm Hg (systolic) in two other subjects and showed no change in others. Finger temperature dropped 1°C ten minutes after beginning of meditation in one case, with no subsequent changes. EEG from right and left motor and occipital lobe showed continuing alpha waves. Low-frequency (6-7 Hz), high-voltage (150-300 μV) brain waves were generally absent.

The GSR increase and respiration decrease were interpreted by the authors as being signs of deep relaxation brought about by meditation. Low-intensity stimuli like taps or noise within 3-5 feet of the meditators sometimes resulted in a GSR change during meditation, but were sometimes ineffective. In one case, no EEG blocking was detected, and twice there was a shift in the baseline of the EEG. The authors suggest that their studies are preliminary and should point the way to new investigations.

4. N. N. Das and H. Gastaut. Variations de l'activite electrique du cerveau, du coeur et des muscles squelletiques au cours de la meditation et de l'extase Yogique. Electroencephalog. Clin. Neurophysiol., Suppl. 6, 211-219 (1955).

This is the only study that mentions high-frequency, low-voltage activity in the brain during meditation. It should be noted that this pattern is typical of the alert human.

5. A. Deikman. Experimental meditation. J. Nervous Mental Disease 136, 329-343 (1963).

A. Deikman. De-automatization and the mystic experience. Psychiatry 29, 324-338 (1966).

Deikman attempted to experimentally produce contemplative meditation. He described the experiences when a subject sits quietly and intently fixates an object, such as a vase. He attempts to relate the observed and reported changes in "mind expansion" and "increased awareness" to emotion and perception variables. He proposes the hypothesis that mystical experiences approximating what have been called samadhi, satori, mind expansion and the like may result from a reversal of normally habituated or "automatized" central nervous system responses to the external and internal milieu.

6. A. Kasamatsu and T. Hirai. An electroencephalographic study on Zen meditation (Zasen). Fol. Psychiat. Neurol. Japan 20, 315-336 (1966).

Measurements were made on Zen Masters during meditation with open eyes. Electroencephalographic records indicate that during Zen meditation, alpha waves appear within a minute or so; the amplitude of the alpha waves increases after about 8-10 minutes, and then the frequency of the waves decreases until theta waves appear after about 24-28 minutes of meditation. The alpha blocking with repeated click stimuli occurred after 3-5 seconds, but no habituation was observed, unlike the control subjects. The authors conclude that the meditational state is unlike sleep or hypnosis.

7. A. Kasamatsu, T. Okuma, S. Takenaka, E. Koga, K. Ikeda and H. Sugiyama. The EEG of Zen and Yoga practitioners. Electroencephalog. Clin. Neurophysiol., Suppl. 9, 51-52 (1957).

The EEGs of two expert practitioners of Zen and Yoga during meditation were compared with those of control subjects while resting. The alpha waves increased remarkably as practitioners progressed into meditation, even if they kept their eyes open. Control subjects had poor alpha waves. Unlike in controls, alpha waves of the Zen and Yoga performers were minimally depressed by the sounds of hand claps or bells.

8. T. Leggett. The Tiger's Cave. Rider and Co., London, 1964.

This book contains an appendix on the physiology of meditation of Kundalini (or Raja) Yoga and Zasen. In Zasen meditating masters, respiration rates were down from 15 to 2-4 per minute. Pulse rates increased as respiration rates decreased. Tidal volume of respiration increased, and oxygen consumption decreased 20-30%.

9. A. Onda. Autogenic training and Zen. In W. Luthe, Ed., Autogenic Training, International Edition. Grune and Stratton, New York, 1965, pp. 251-258.

Onda has compared autogenic training and Zen. He says that both autogenic training and Zen developed from and are analogous to some yoga practices; therefore, it would appear that both are related to yoga. He reported, however, that autogenic training and Zen have both similarities and differences.

10. C. Tart, Ed. Altered States of Consciousness. John Wiley & Sons, New York, 1969.

This book contains very readable and informative chapters on the physiology of Zen and yogi meditation, autogenic training, and operant control of brain waves.

11. B. Timmons and J. Kamiya. The psychology of meditation and related phenomena: a bibliography. J. Transpersonal Psychol. 2, 41-59 (1970).

A bibliography of articles on the psychophysiology of meditation, primarily the practice of Buddhism and yoga. The period covered ranges from about 1925 through 1969, although some publications that were in preparation in 1969 are included. About 320 titles are listed. This bibliography is a good starting point for researchers doing work in this field. It includes five references on TM. (For a sequel to this bibliography, see p. 141.)

V. The Psychobiology of Wakefulness, Deep Sleep, and Dreaming

1. D. Foulkes. The Psychology of Sleep. Charles Scribner and Sons,
    New York, 1966.

    This book deals mostly with the psychological and behavioral effects
    of sleep and dreaming. It also contains some supporting physio-
    logical data.

2. E. Hartman. The Biology of Dreaming. Charles C. Thomas, Spring-
    field, Illinois, 1967.(See also p. 51 for a later book by author.)

    This book contains tables listing the physiological correlates of
    the wakeful, dreaming, and deep-sleep states. Preceded in 1958
    by W. C. Dement's Ph.D. thesis on the subject.

3. D. Kleitman. Sleep and Wakefulness. Revised and enlarged edition.
    University of Chicago Press, Chicago, Illinois, 1963.

    A good beginning reference book on sleep. It also contains chapters
    on hypnotism and hibernation, and a long list of references.

4. G. G. Luce. Current Research on Sleep and Dreams. Publ. No. 1389,
    Public Health Service, U.S. Department of Health, Education and
    Welfare. U.S. Government Printing Office, Washington, D.C. 20402
    (1965).

    A review and explanation of research on sleep and dreaming written
    for the nonspecialist.

5. G. G. Luce. Biological Rhythems in Human and Animal Physiology.
    Dover Publications, New York, 1971. Originally published under the
    title Biological Rhythms in Psychiatry and Medicine, Publ. No. 2088,
    Public Health Service, U.S. Department of Health, Education and
    Welfare (1970).

    An up-to-date book on the subject written for the nonspecialist and
    based on the latest scientific findings.

6. G. G. Luce and J. Segal. Sleep. Lancer Books, New York, 1967.

    Explains in laymen' language what is known about the psychophysiology
    of sleep and dreaming and the effects of drugs thereon; describes
    abnormalities in sleep.

114

7. A. Rechtschaffen and A. Kales, Eds. A Manual of Standardized Ter-
minology, Techniques and Scoring System for Sleep Stages of Human
Subjects. Publ. No. 204, Public Health Service, U.S. Government
Printing Office, Washington, D. C., 1968.

Contains actual EEG, EOG and EMG recordings of three young normal
male college students as they progressed through the different
stages of sleep, and schematic diagrams thereof. About 30 pages
of full-page recordings and a discussion of terminology.

8. F. Snyder. Psychophysiology of human sleep. Clin. Neurosurg. <u>18</u>,
503-536 (1971).

A review article on the subject of sleep. Deep sleep is characterized by hypofunction of almost every physiological bodily function.
Vasodilation and vasoconstriction alternate at approximately hourly
intervals. When subjects were awakened from REM sleep, 60 to 90%
reported dreams. When they were awakened from non-REM sleep, the
results were rather inconsistent: 0 to 70% reported brief, frag-
mentary descriptions of thoughts (some mental activity), not entire-
ly resembling reports during "dreaming." All land mammals tested
have periods resembling human REM sleep. The largest proportion of
REM was found in the opossum, which has the least developed brain
of animals tested. During REM sleep (the dreaming state), (1) vasoconstriction takes place; (2) O_2 and CO_2 increase slightly; (3) systolic blood pressure rises and fluctuates, and breathing and pulse
rates become highly irregular; (4) gastric peristalsis is that of
waking; (5) spinal fluid pressures increase, often ranging up to
twice the baseline found in other stages of sleep.

During non-REM sleep (the deep-sleep state), average changes of
physiological parameters are (1) O_2 consumption gradually drops,
with minimum decrease (11.5%) after about six hours of sleep; (2)
rectal temperature gradually decreases, reaching a minimum after
about 5-6 hours (down about $1.75^{\circ}C$); (3) respiration rate gradually
decreases (from 18 to 15 breaths per minute in six hours); (4) heart
rate decreases (from 62 to 50 beats per minute in 4-5 hours); (5)
skin temperature first increases slightly during the first hour or
so and then gradually decreases (down $0.5-0.75^{\circ}C$); (6) systolic blood
pressure decreases (drops abruptly) during the first 1.5 hours (by
about 10%), then increases over several hours (by about 15-20%; (7)
alveolar pCO_2 first increases (by about 10%) and then decreases
later in sleep (by about 10-12%); and (8) body movement first decreases and then gradually increases. Similar changes in the first
four body measures can be produced by sustained bodily rest and relaxation. (Contains 140 references.)

VI. Biofeedback and Yoga and Other Exercises

1. T. Barber, L. DiCara, J. Kamiya, N. Miller, D. Shapiro and J. Stoyva, Eds. Biofeedback and Self-control, A Reader. Aldine-Atherton, Chicago, Illinois, 1971.

2. T. Barber, L. DiCara, J. Kamiya, N. Miller, D. Shapiro and J. Stoyva, Eds. Biofeedback and Self-control 1970, An Aldine Annual. Aldine-Atherton, Chicago, Illinois, 1971.

3. J. Stoyva, T. Barber, L. V. DiCara, J. Kamiya, N. E. Miller, and D. Shapiro, Eds. Biofeedback and Self-control 1971, An Aldine Annual. Aldine-Atherton, Chicago, Illinois, 1972.

4. D. Shapiro, T. Barber, L. V. DiCara, J. Kamiya, N. E. Miller, and J. Stoyva, Eds. Biofeedback and Self-control 1972, An Aldine Annual. Aldine-Atherton, Chicago, Illinois, 1973.

The above four books deal with the regulation of bodily processes and topics of consciousness. They are the first source books in the field of biofeedback.

5. A. Caycedo. India of Yogis. National Publishing House, Delhi, India, 1966.

Dr. Caycedo founded Sophrology, a school. He set up the school with other psychiatrists and psychologists interested in using all techniques in which the change of the state of consciousness is of fundamental importance. Dr. Caycedo toured India for two years, interviewing various yogis and visiting laboratories and clinics where the various medical aspects of yoga are studied by Indian doctors. He presents the data from these interviews--he says with complete neutrality. This book may be considered as an introduction to the various practices of yogis and to the attempts to scientifically investigate their effectiveness as psychosomatic therapy.

6. K. H. Cooper. Aerobics. Bantom Book No. PS 3911, 1968.

The "training effect" of physical exercise is most efficiently brought about when exercise is vigorous enough to sustain a heart rate of about 150 beats per minute and the oxygen consumption is about twice normal, i.e., during jogging, swimming, cycling, etc. Cooper suggests that the "training effect" not only includes improvement in efficiency of lungs and heart (blood circulation) and in muscle tone, bringing about a well-coordinated body, but also changes the outlook on life, induces relaxation, develops a better self-image, and enables the exerciser to better tolerate the stress of daily living.

7. K. K. Datey, S. N. Deshmukh, C. P. Dalvi and S. L. Vinekar. "Shavasan": A yogic exercise in the management of hypertension. Angiology 20, 325-333 (1969).

Datey et al. used yogic breathing exercises to reduce breathing rates (from 22 to 8 breaths per minute in one subject), to produce muscular quiescence (EMG from the frontalis muscle reduced almost to zero in one case), and to reduce the blood pressure and, it appears, the amount of antihypertensive drugs used by 47 chronic hypertensive patients. About half of the patients showed some response. One reduced her blood pressure from 180/110 to 110/70 in 38 weeks. The average systolic blood pressure reduction was about 20%, with a corresponding decrease in the diastolic blood pressure ($p < .05$). Some subjects who showed no response had arteriosclerosis or did not perform the exercise regularly. The exercise was performed for 30 minutes daily. The etiology of the hypertension was essential (32 cases), renal (12 cases), and arteriosclerotic (3 cases). The group consisted of 37 men and 10 women 22 to 64 years old (average of 46 years). Their original systolic blood pressure ranged from 160 to 270 mm Hg, and the diastolic from 90 to 145 mm Hg (average 186/115 mm Hg).

8. E. E. Green, E. D. Walters, A. M. Green and G. Murphy. Feedback technique for deep relaxation. Psychophysiology 6, 371-377 (1969).

A discussion of the use of biofeedback techniques in humans. The authors provided feedback reflecting muscle potentials. They found that in many of the subjects, muscle potentials attained levels near zero.

9. E. Jacobson. Modern Treatment of Tense Patients. Charles C. Thomas, Springfield, Illinois, 1970.

The author proposes that brain, nerves and muscles act together as a unit. No thinking or emotions occur without neuromuscular effects. Conversely, muscular activity is accompanied by mental activity. Relaxation of muscles tensed by anxiety relieves that anxiety.

Jacobson gives detailed instructions on how to become familiar with sensations of different muscles. The book also summarizes most of the material provided in previous publications by the author, the more important of which are Progressive Relaxation (University of Chicago Press, 1938) and Anxiety and Tension Control (Lippincott, Philadelphia, 1964).

10. J. Kamiya. Conscious control of brain waves. Psychol. Today 1, 57-60 (April 1968).

   Kamiya was the first to show, in systematic studies, that humans can control their brain waves by means of biofeedback. Particular brain wave states (e.g., predominance of alpha or theta waves) could be readily learned by most subjects. These brain wave states were also frequently associated with relatively discrete "feeling" states of relaxation or increased awareness.

11. P. V. Karambelkar, M. V. Bhole and M. L. Gharote. Effect of yogic asanas on uropepsin excretion. Indian J. Med. Res. 57, 944-947 (1969).

   "A close relationship between the excretion of uropepsin and adrenal cortical function has been postulated by several workers. The activity of the adrenal cortex is supposed to be modified in a variable manner by different yoga practices, depending on their psychophysiological mechanisms. This paper reports the effects of daily practice of yoga asanas." (Authors' abstract.)

   Fifteen males (18 to 43 years old) and five females (26 to 27 years old) served as the experimental group. Eleven males (18 to 45 years) and five females (25 to 26 years) constituted the control group. Uropepsin excretion was reduced significantly in the experimental group of students after three weeks of 1.5 hours of yoga postures daily (p < .001). The control group of students, who had a similar diet and school load but who did not perform yoga asanas, showed less of a decrease in uropepsin excretion (p < .100).

12. N. E. Miller. Learning visceral and glandular responses. Science 163, 434-445 (1969).

   Animals can be taught to control autonomic nervous system functions (e.g., regional blood flow, heart rate, blood pressure) by use of an instrumental reward and punishment method. Miller speculates on the implications of this control on human behavior and health.

13. K. R. Pelletier. Psychophysiological parameters of the voluntary control of blood flow and pain. Paper presented at the Western Psychological Association Meetings, San Francisco, April 1974.

   "For over eight centuries, meditators have claimed to be capable of autonomic control of heart rate, pain, and blood flow. Investigations of these abilities have been inconclusive with little attempt to monitor how certain brain wave modulation might mediate such control. To answer these questions, research concerning alpha, theta, and autonomic control was conducted with a single subject, Jack Schwarz, using an intensive, repeated measures design. Alpha and theta enhancement was monitored on a number of psychophysiological parameters in order to determine how these states might be differentiated. Secondly, these same variables were monitored while the subject demonstrated the voluntary control of bleeding and pain.

"All testing was conducted during a one-week period in Dr. Joe Kamiya's Psychophysiology Laboratory, Langley Porter Neuropsychiatric Institute. Experimentation was conducted in a shielded, sound-proof room with two physicians in attendance at all times. Indices monitored were: 1) left central alpha; 2) left occipital alpha; 3) left central theta; 4) left occipital theta; 5) EKG and cardio-tachometer; 6) integrated EMG; 7) reset integrated EMG; 8) transient electrodermal response; 9) basal electrodermal response; 10) thoracic respiration rate and pattern; 11) abdominal respiration rate and pattern; and 12) clinical interviews. These indices were recorded while the subject received alpha or theta feedback during 100 two-minute sessions of alpha and during 100 two-minute sessions of theta. On four occasions, the subject pierced his left bicep with a sharpened, unsterilized knitting needle and demonstrated the voluntary control of bleeding and pain.

"All indices registered a differentiation of alpha and theta at the .05 level or better. On four occasions, the subject did control bleeding and pain from a self-induced puncture completely through the medial aspect of his left upper arm. Alpha production appeared to mediate the autonomic control achieved during the puncture demonstrations.

"Conclusion and Implications: Alpha and theta can be differentiated as discrete states and voluntary control of cardiovascular functions can be achieved. Implications of this and future research were discussed in terms of psychosomatic medicine, instrumentation of altered states of consciousness, and applications in biofeedback-based psychotherapy." (Author's abstract.)

14. F. N. Pitts, Jr. The biochemistry of anxiety. Scientific American 220(2), 69-76 (1969).

"Patients with anxiety neurosis show an excessive rise in lactate, a normal metabolic product. A double-blind experiment has shown that anxiety symptoms and attacks can be induced by infusion." (Author's abstract.)

Lactic acid level is positively correlated with fatigue, and it has been reported that cadaveral rigidity in overfatigued soldiers and athletes can be attributed to large increases of lactic acid in the blood. Persons suffering from anxiety neurosis produce more lactic acid than nonanxious persons do, and infusion of lactic acid has been reported to produce anxiety-like symptoms.

15. A. Weil. The Natural Mind. Houghton Mifflin, 1973.

   Dr. Weil, an M.D. pharmacologist, views drugs as one way of achieving
   altered states of consciousness that are more satisfyingly achieved
   by meditation. He postulates an inherent drive in humans to achieve
   altered states of consciousness.

16. J. White. The Highest State of Consciousness. Anchor-Doubleday,
    New York, 1972.

   Mr. White is a free-lance writer. This paperback contains an extensive collection of readings about altered states of consciousness,
   including a section on TM.

VII. Research Coordination

   Information on research studies on TM is made available through
several coordinating centers in Europe and the United States. These
centers are kept informed of all new studies on TM, both in their area
and world-wide. They provide, to interested persons, reprints of papers
and other information on TM research projects and publications. SIMS
Los Angeles keeps a current list (called the Scientists' Index) of active
scientists doing TM research.

   Listed below are names and addresses of those responsible for these
coordinating centers:

Philip C. Ferguson, M.A.
Director
MIU International Center for Scientific Research
1015 Gayley Avenue
Los Angeles, California 90024

Dr. Anthony Campbell
2, Bishopswood Road
London N.6, England

Dipl. Phys. K.-D. Kniffki
MIU-Maharishi International University
FRSI-Forschungsring
D-3000 Hannover, Gretchen Str. 36, Germany

   This organization publishes a monthly literature survey
   (Schöpferische Intelligenz e.v.) listing the articles published
   on TM and related subjects.

Appendix B

STEPS PRESCRIBED TO LEARN THE TECHNIQUE
OF TRANSCENDENTAL MEDITATION

Appendix B

STEPS PRESCRIBED TO LEARN THE TECHNIQUE
OF TRANSCENDENTAL MEDITATION

A nonprofit organization, the Students' International Meditation Society (SIMS) and its affiliate[†],the International Meditation Society (IMS), have been set up to teach TM. All the teachers certified by SIMS-IMS have been trained by Maharishi Mahesh Yogi. Thus, what is taught and the instructional methods used are uniform throughout the many meditation centers in the world. Headquarters of SIMS-IMS are at 1015 Gayley Avenue, Los Angeles, California 90024.

Steps of Learning

Described below is the sequence of events that a prospective meditator goes through before and during the early stages of learning the technique of TM. It should be noted, parenthetically, that subsequent to the above events and after some period of continued practice of TM, the practitioner may study to become an instructor or may participate in TM seminars during which extended and advanced knowledge about TM is taught. Advanced courses in TM are available as part of certain optional programs.

1. First Introductory Lecture

   In the course of a 60- to 90-minute lecture, a general description of the physiological and psychological changes that appear to result from practice of TM is provided. At this lecture, much of the information described above is discussed--to a greater or lesser extent, depending on the apparent interest of and the questions from the audience.

2. Second Introductory Lecture

   At this time, the principles and mechanics of the technique are described and an outline of the program to follow is given. In addition, the instructor gives a brief historical account of the movement and its scope.

3. Interview

   Immediately following the second lecture, interested individuals fill out an application form and meet with the instructor for a personal interview to check the contents of the form. An appointment for personal instruction is then made.

[†]See Footnote p. 125.

4. Initial Learning and Practice of TM ("Personal Instruction")

Learning the technique and checking with the instructor to assure
that it is being practiced correctly requires a total time of about
six hours over four consecutive days.

(a) First day. On the first convenient* day following the second
lecture, the instructor performs and the student is a witness
to a brief private ceremony honoring the long tradition of
masters who have kept the teachings intact to this day. This
ceremony is performed in front of a picture of the latest of
these teachers of TM, Guru Dev. After this ceremony, the instructor discloses the student's mantra. The selected mantra
is one of several that have a resonant quality and that apparently have been found, after centuries of use, to be effective
in directing perception and thinking inwardly. The mantra is
a Sanskrit word whose quality is employed only--not its meaning.
Brief instructions are given as to how to think or, more accu-
rately, experience the mantra, and a brief period (10 to 20
minutes) of practice by the student is permitted. Subsequently, the instructor determines whether the experiences of the
student during the meditation period indicate that his practice
was within normal limits; if they were not, he guides the student to correct the practice. Another practice session may
ensue and more suggestions may be made, if required. This personal instruction, which takes approximately 40 to 45 minutes,
ensures that the practice is correct.

(b) Second day. The person meditates for about 15 to 20 minutes in
the morning and in the evening. In the evening, or at some
other convenient time, he comes to the first group meeting to
discuss his experiences** during meditation and to be given
further instructions about the technique. The session lasts
about 1-1½ hours.

(c) Third day. The person continues to practice the technique, and
in the evening comes to a second group meeting for further instructions based on his experiences. The mechanics of stress
release are explained at this time. The session lasts about
1-1½ hours.

---

*Subject is asked to abstain from taking any nonprescribed drugs for 15
days prior to personal instruction. If a person has taken nonprescribed
drugs, he is asked to wait for instruction until the required time has
elapsed.

**During the individual and group instruction, attention is restricted to
the mechanics of the practice itself. No other subjects are discussed,
nor is there any counseling on personal matters outside the practice
itself.

(d) <u>Fourth day</u>. The person continues to practice the technique regularly and in the evening comes to a third group meeting for completion of his instructions, again based on his experiences. A "vision of possibilities" for development of full potential of the individual is also discussed. A personal interview with the initiator follows this meeting. This session (group and interview) may require about 2 hours.

(e) <u>Regular checking</u>. After about 10-14 days of regular individual practice, the person meets privately with the instructor for about one-half hour to check his practice of meditation. Subsequent individual "checking" of the practice is recommended about once a month for the first year of practice.

(f) <u>Group meetings</u>. Optional weekly group meetings are available to clarify experiences and give further intellectual understanding of the technique.

Organization Teaching Transcendental Meditation

Students' International Meditation Society
International Meditation Society
1015 Gayley Avenue
Los Angeles, California 90024
(213) 477-4537

Area and regional coordinating centers of SIMS/IMS can be reached by writing to the above address.

For maximum results one should not try to practice TM by himself without having gone first through a regular course conducted by a qualified TM teacher. The TM technique though natural and simple is very delicate. It definitely should be learned properly from a TM teacher going through the seven basic steps described above.

+ Since the report was published, the following three organizations have been set up to teach TM, train teachers, conduct research, etc.: Maharishi International University (MIU); American Foundation for the Science of Creative Intelligence (AFSCI); and Spiritual Regeneration Movement (SRM).

Appendix C

SELECTED TESTIMONIALS

Appendix C

SELECTED TESTIMONIALS

Some positive subjective effects as well as some pronounced changes in behavior that have accompanied the practice of TM are illustrated by the following statements selected from "TM, Some Results" (Anonymous, 1969) and some unsolicited correspondence to D. P. Kanellakos.

- F, 22, student, 16 months*: "In April 1966 I had to leave college to enter a mental hospital. I was hypertense, overemotional, self-destructive and was putting on weight extremely fast. I left the hospital not really able to function or to relate to reality at all. For a year or two I lived alone and took a lot of drugs--put on 35 pounds in less than three months. After that I was never able to lose the weight as it was a result of tension as well as of an emptiness inside. I did not know myself, I did not respect myself, and felt that anything that happened to me didn't matter--if it was bad, fine--if good, I destroyed it because I felt I was not worth it. I really feel I was very sick for a long time after I left the hospital. In February 1968-- after almost 2 years of doing nothing--I began TM. Within 3 months I lost over 30 pounds and felt physically and mentally as if I were able to move again. I was able to be with people, to begin to have some self-respect, and to have circumstances work out for me--the support of nature. Last February I returned to school, came out first in all but one class and had to do very little work even so. I feel great about everything--there are still hassles and some uncertainty but I feel confident about my ability to do whatever is necessary and to enjoy a lot of it. Actually I can't really remember what it was like to be so unhappy and incompetent and I don't think much about it now. I expect that everything will keep improving as it has.

  "This sounds a bit dramatic but I feel that the benefits I have received through meditation are more than dramatic--to my family, it is almost incredible."

- M, craftsman, 17 months: "Before I started TM I was a quite happy person and seemed to find success in whatever I did. The only area of my being with which I found dissatisfaction was that large and most important, though very subtle area of my personal insight into myself (and others). Since beginning TM I have become satisfied in this area and am becoming ever more satisfied. This is not to deny that there are other changes as well; indeed my brother claims to see as dramatic

---

* (M) male, (F) female; age; occupation; duration of practice of TM.

changes in me as I see in him, and I fully believe him, but it is on the level of personal insight that I am most appreciative of the effects of TM on me."

- M, student, 8 months: "Before I began meditation, I was much less tolerant of other people, and I was very nervous and easily upset.

  "Now, after meditating eight months, I find that I get along better with people. Problems confronting me do not seem to bother me as much as they used to; I am able to face my problems and solve them more efficiently rather than worry about them. I have found that learning is easier; since I began meditating my semester grade point average has risen from 2.6 to 3.4."

- F, 36, housewife, 14 months: "Before I started meditating, I smoked fairly heavily (tobacco). Now I don't smoke at all. I quit easily, without any effort, and without even realizing I was doing so at first, gradually over a year's time. I also drank alcohol at parties. Now I never do, for through meditation I could feel that it was damaging. I knew this before, although more vaguely, but could not stop when it was socially expected, but after meditating a year I found I could easily enjoy myself in any social situation without such crutches. I have a natural strength of my own convictions. I was very ill with arthritis. For years no doctor has been able to help it much, and I was depressed because of the vision of a future of increasing illness. Gradually, through meditation, I have been getting better! I no longer need to use any drugs to help it, and have almost no arthritic symptoms! This is partially due to the relaxing benefits of meditation directly, but mainly it is due to better eating habits. However, these better eating habits are due to the increased energy, persistence, good spirits, and intelligence put to use in the search for knowledge in the field of nutrition. . . . I am still amazed at the knowledge I have amassed this year, and the energy and determination put into it. A year ago, before meditating, I would not have been able to do it! In addition the search was wonderful fun. . .!

  "I hated cooking before, and was too tired to do a good job of it for my family. Now I'm an excellent cook, love it, and have energy sufficient for it; good meals appear almost by themselves. This still amazes me at times. For the first time in my married life I am enjoying my role and responsibilities as a cook, wife, mother, housewife—and mainly because of my good self-image due to my new capabilities and accomplishments. Our family used to argue a lot; now we don't. We speak more softly, with more love and understanding, patience. We enjoy each other more. The children have benefitted so much, it still seems miraculous. I am less shy than before; more sure of myself and the value of my opinions, convictions. I listen better to other people, an very much more interested in what they have to say. My visual (and sometimes auditory) perceptions are much clearer, and I enjoy scenery more than I ever have before (although I always have loved natural scenery).

130

I am attracted instantly, often, by the smallest and most intricate and lovely patterns in nature, that formerly I missed."

- F: "I have experienced a spectacular (to me) change and have often thought of telling a doctor about it but thought they would feel it was a bit far-fetched unless, of course, they were meditators, too. So you can see I was pleased to find out that you were doing research in this area. I have been meditating for a little over two years and after a little less than one year of practicing TM I discovered I had cured a small duodenal ulcer that I had had for some years. I have never bothered to have an X-ray to prove that it is healed but I can eat anything I want and have not had an attack in over a year. The only thing I can attribute this to is TM because that is the only change I had made in my way of life." (February 1970)

- M: "Regarding TM: In the fall of 1968, I became emotionally disturbed and by the spring of 1969, after being hospitalized and seeing two psychiatrists, I was taking amphetamines, but I was unable to function on a job. In August of 1969, I stopped taking the medicine because it was making a physical wreck of me. In September I was initiated and began to meditate. I'm now relaxed and unworried with more calmness and energy than I ever had under the effects of the amphetamines. The meditation seems to give me much the same exhilaration and fearlessness as the medicine. I'm not in psychotherapy now and I'm working. I hope this is of interest to you." (December 1969)

- F: "I was suffering from epileptic attacks two or three times a day, three or four times a week. Then in March 1969 I began to meditate. By midsummer I was taking less and less antiepileptic drugs which are very expensive. Since mid-July I have not been taking any medication and I have had no epileptic attacks. I have not told my doctor of my stopping taking these drugs; he would not believe me." (December 1969)

- F: "I was suffering from angina. I was sleeping many more hours a day than my husband. I was taking nitroglycerine tablets for my pain. Then I began to meditate. After a few weeks my pains were reduced, I stopped taking medication, my sleeping hours were reduced, and I have more energy." (October 1969)

- F: "I was suffering from high blood pressure. After I began to meditate, my blood pressure began to drop until after a few months when it was normal again." (June 1969)

- M: "Since I began to meditate (May 1969), I have become less violent; I have grown more serene and have given and received more smiles than I ever remember. My capacity to love has increased and the relationships with the other members of my family have greatly improved. Even though the output of my work has increased (I spent more time at my

131

desk working than before), I feel less strain performing it. My intuition and knowledge of myself has increased: I love myself more, my self-esteem has gone up and my self-confidence has increased. I sleep less hours per night, yet I awake refreshed in the mornings. The quality of my dreaming has changed (a disturbing repetitive dream disappeared and most of my dreams are not confused or disturbing as before). More now than ever I know what I want from life and where I am going. I am more alert of what's happening in my environment. My senses have been refined and I am aware of more things about me. My taste for food has changed to more and more natural foods and it takes me longer to eat less food than before. I have greatly reduced the use of alcohol and tobacco; they have become unpleasant in taste or produce no effects. I am deepening my knowledge of my religion. I am much calmer and less things bother me than before. I feel lighter in mind and body (many hang-ups which bothered me have now left me) and I run longer distances at shorter times; (reduced my four mile record by 12 percent) and with less effort. I have grown more tolerant of others and a lot of my prejudices have been either eliminated or reduced. I am developing a capacity to see an integral picture from examining or looking at the various seemingly unrelated parts. My professional tendencies are now directed towards uncovering as much as possible of the biology of meditation and developing applications of some of these biological changes for developing latent internal resources of individuals." (May 1970)

• Observations on TM by M. K. Bowers, M.D., F.A.P.A., 4 Grove Street, New York, N.Y. 10014: "In the past two years I have been able to persuade about 30 of my patients to start TM. Most of them have been pleased and have continued to meditate. Quite a number have refused to go into TM. With some of these there is a fear of introspection; an unwillingness to help themselves; disbelief; fear of being taken over by hostile forces, etc. Two patients have been unable to continue TM because of the intrusion of severely disturbing thoughts. Some have been unable or unwilling to adopt a routine of meditation as a discipline. A large proportion have required encouragement, especially when bothered by unstressing. One of these required daily checking for several weeks before she could meditate alone on a regular basis. Others have had no problems.

"All who have persevered with TM have shown a much faster rate of improvement in the course of psychotherapy. With several this improvement has been dramatic, even spectacular. Some have been relieved of symptoms that had never been helped by psychotherapy. With two such patients this relief and general improvement, increase in ego-strength, general productivity at work and happiness in living have continued with greatly decreased hours of psychotherapy. With every patient who has been faithful in TM, the improvement has been at least twice the expected rate (as judged by previous experience with the patient). Sometimes it seems to be at least 10 times the expected rate. Sometimes when a patient complains about not moving at a satisfactory rate, I find that the patient has stopped TM. When TM is again undertaken, movement picks up again.

"With TM, most patients need fewer hours of psychotherapy and the sessions are more meaningful and useful.

"Frequently TM becomes the principal therapy. Psychotherapy sessions become secondary and are useful in the understanding of bothersome unstressing, or can be understood as just talking things over with an old friend."

Appendix D

MISCELLANEOUS SCIENTIFIC AND POPULAR REPORTS

Appendix D

MISCELLANEOUS SCIENTIFIC AND POPULAR REPORTS

Anonymous. Physiologic changes during Transcendental Meditation. Connecticut Medicine 34, 302-303 (1970).

Anonymous. Transzendetale Meditation. Münchener Medizinische Wochen-schrift 112, 1-4 (1970); Aktuelle Medizin No. 32.

Anonymous. Meditation can be scientific. New Scientist, p. 501 (May 1973).

Anonymous. Alpha biofeedback: making waves in self-treatment. Special Roche Report, Frontiers of Psychiatry 4(1), 1, 2, 11 (January 1, 1974) (Nutley, New Jersey 07110).

H. Benson, J. F. Beary and M. P. Carol. The relaxation response. Psychiatry 37, 37-46 (1974).

H. Benson and L. S. King. Transcendental Meditation—science or cult? J. Am. Med. Assoc. 227, No. 7 (February 18, 1974).

H. Benson, B. P. Malvea and J. R. Graham. Physiologic correlates of meditation and their clinical effects in headache: An ongoing investigation. Headache 13, 23-24 (1973).

H. Benson, B. A. Rosner, B. Marzetta and H. Klemback. Decreased blood-pressure in pharmacologically treated hypertensive patients who regularly elicited the relaxation response. The Lancet 1, No. 7852, 289-291 (February 23, 1974).

N. Blücher. Transzendentale Meditation nach Maharishi Mahesh Yogi. In Wege der Meditation Hente, Herausgeber: U. V. Mangoldt, O. W. Barth (Verlag, Welheim, 1970).

D. Bright, V. Buccola, W. Stone and J. Toohey. What physicians, nurses and health educators should know about Transcendental Meditation. J. School Health 43, 192-194 (March 1973).

J. Brooks. Transcendental Meditation and its potential role in clinical medicine, The Synapse 1, No. 3 (School of Medicine, Wayne State University, Detroit, Michigan, December 7, 1973).

J. Camp. Think deep, think happy, think healthy. World Medicine 8(25), 15-23 (Sept. 5, 1973).

A. Campbell, Ed. Towards pinning down meditation. Hospital Times, London, May 1, 1970.

A. Campbell. Seven States of Consciousness. Victor Gollanez, Ltd., London, 1973. (Harper and Row, 1974.)

C. Campbell. The facts on Transcendental Meditation. Part I. Transcendence is as American as Ralph Waldo Emerson. Psychology Today 7(11), 37-38 (April 1974).

G. Chedd. Mental medicine: self-help for your insides? New Scientist 51, 560 -563 (1971).

D. Clutterbuck. How I learned to stop worrying and love the job. International Management, 27-29 (August 1973).

J. E. Coleman. Transcendental Meditation versus "Pot." In The Quiet Mind, Harper & Row, New York, 1971, pp 170-186.

R. W. Collier. Extraordinary states of consciousness: implications of some recent experiments for the field of language learning. Proc. Pacific Northwest Conference on Foreign Languages, Seattle, 1973 (in press).

V. H. Dhanaraj. Effect of yoga and the 5BX fitness plan as selected physiological parameters, Exercise Physiology (Faculty of Physical Education, University of Alberta, Edmonton, Alberta, Canada, (1973).

F. G. Driscoll. TM as a secondary school subject. Phi Delta Kappan 54(4), 236-237 (December 1972).

M. Eastman. The military meditators. Family: Army Times, July 4, 1973.

P. Fenwick. The neurophysiology of meditation. Intellectual Digest 3, 34 (November 1973).

P. C. Ferguson and J. C. Gowan. TM--some preliminary psychological findings, J. Humanistic Psychol. (in press).

M. Glickman. Transcendental Meditation. Physicians World, p. 10, August 1973.

D. Goleman. Meditation and stress reactivity. Ph.D. thesis, 1973-1974, Department of Social Relations, Harvard University.

K. Goodall. Meditation as a drug-trip detour. Psychology Today, March 1972.

138

F. Griffith. Meditation research: its personal and social implications. In Frontiers of Consciousness, J. White, Ed., Julian Press, New York, 1974.

D. Haddon. New plant thrives in a spiritual desert. Christianity Today 18(6), 9-12 (December 21, 1973).

J. Hart. The Zen of Hubert Benoit. J. Transpersonal Psychol. 2(2), 141-167 (1970).

C. Howard. A magical concoction or just another fad? Scholastic Teacher, April 1973, pp 25-26.

H. H. Hussey, Ed. Meditation may find use in medical practice. J. Am. Med. Assoc. 219, 295-299 (January 17, 1972).

C. Kanellakos. Transcendental Meditation: what its all about. Scholastic Coach 43(7), 48 (1974).

D. P. Kanellakos. Transcendental Meditation and the psychobiology of consciousness. In Proceedings First International Symposium on the Science of Creative Intelligence, University of Massachusetts, Amherst, Massachusetts, July 1971.

D. P. Kanellakos. Thinking away fatigue. Runner's World Magazine 9(6), 4 (June 1973).

D. P. Kanellakos and P. C. Ferguson, Eds. The Psychobiology of Transcendental Meditation (An Annotated Bibliography). MIU Press, 1015 Gayley Avenue, Los Angeles, California 90024, Spring 1973, 28 pp.

P. Kaplan and S. Kaplan. Transcendental Meditation: its value in optometry. Optometric Weekly, November 22, 1973.

V. Katz. Some basic insights of the present revival. Creative Intelligence 1(1) (1971).

P. Keil, Ed., California Business. Business and Financial Newsweekly of the West, January 4, 1971.

K.-D. Kniffki. Transzendentale Meditation unter den kritischen Augen der Wissenschaft. Nds. Ärzteblatt 44, 404 (1971).

K.-D. Kniffki, Ed. Schöpferische Intelligence, 1972, 1973, 1974. (Monthly newsletter in German on TM and related literature obtained from D-3000 Hannover, Gretchenstrasse 36, Germany.)

K.-D. Kniffki. Transzendentale Meditation. Goldmann Toschenbücher-Medizin, No. 9017, Vorankündigüng, 1973.

D. Larsen. Meditation for managers. Industry Week 178(6), 37-40 (August 6, 1973).

H. J. Laue. The science of creative intelligence and management science. Presented at the Eighth International Symposium on the Science of Creative Intelligence, California State University at Humboldt, August 29, 1972, and at the Symposium on the Science of Creative Intelligence, Rensselaer Polytechnic Institute, Hartford, Connecticut, March 13, 1973.

G. LeDain et al. Treatment. In A Report of the Commission of Inquiry into the Nonmedical Use of Drugs, pp 99-101, Information Canada, Ottawa, Canada, 1972.

V. L. Levander, H. Benson, R. C. Wheeler and R. K. Wallace. Increased forearm blood flow during a wakeful hypometabolic state. Fed. Proc. 31, 405 (1972)(Abstract).

P. H. Levine. Transcendental Meditation and the Science of Creative Intelligence. Phi Delta Kappan 54(4), 231-236 (December 1972).

R. N. Livingstone. Business tries meditating. The New Englander, June 1973, pp 19-22.

D. Mallicoat. Consciousness 4--it probes the inner core of being. Soldiers: Official U.S. Army Magazine 27(2) (February 1972).

J. Marcus. Transcendental Meditation: a new method of reducing drug abuse. Drug Forum 3(2) (Winter 1973).

G. R. MacIntosh. Transcendental Meditation and Selected Life Attitudes. M.A. Thesis, School of Social Welfare, University of Calgary, Alberta, Canada, February, 1972

B. Muller. Bericht über die Meditationswochen. Elmauer Blätter 21 (1), 29-30 (June 1972).

R. Ornstein. The Nature of Human Consciousness: A Book of Readings. Viking, Freeman, New York, 1973.

R. Ornstein. The Psychology of Consciousness. Viking, Freeman, New York, 1973.

L. S. Otis. The facts on Transcendental Meditation. Part III. If well-integrated but anxious, try TM. Psychology Today 7(11), 45-46 (April 1974).

K. R. Pelletier. Neurological, psychophysiological and clinical differentiation of the "alpha" and "theta" altered states of consciousness: voluntary control of bleeding and pain. Ph.D. thesis, 1973, Psychology Clinic, University of California, Berkeley, California.

H. Rieckert. Plethysmographische Untersuchungen bei Konzentrations und Meditationsübungen. Arztlische Forsch. 21, 61-65 (1967).

B. Romano. Transcendental Meditation: philosophical and physiological aspects. Ph.D. dissertation, 1970, Department of Philosophy, University of Rome, Rome, Italy (in Italian).

T. Schaertel. Transcendental Meditation. Student Impact, pp 12-13, 17 (November 1972). (Student National Educational Association, 1201 Sixteenth Street N.W., Washington, D. C. 20036.)

T. Schultz. What science is discovering about the potential benefits of meditation. Today's Health 50(4) ,36 (April 1972).

G. E. Schwartz. The facts on Transcendental Meditation. Part II. TM relaxes some people and makes them feel better. Psychology Today 7(11), 39-44 (April 1974).

S. H. Scott. Mind over matter. Mensa Journal 141, 4 (December 1970).

M. W. Shelly. The theory of happiness as it relates to Transcendental Meditation. Department of Psychology, University of Kansas, Lawrence, Kansas. [Summary of section in Sources of Satisfaction, University of Kansas Press, Lawrence, Kansas, 1973, and The Counter-Evolution, 1973 (in press).]

D. D. Simpson, D. F. Dancereau and G. Giles. A Preliminary Evaluation of the Effects of Self-directed Relaxation. Behavior Research Laboratory, Texas Christian University, Forth Worth, Texas; IBR Technical Report No. 71-12, NASA Grant NGR-009-008, September 1971.

B. Timmons and D. P. Kanellakos. The psychology and physiology of meditation and related phenomena: a bibliography. II. J. Transpersonal Psychol. 6(1) (1974).

A. S. Tjoa. The effects of Transcendental Meditation on neuroticism and intelligence. Unpublished report from the Psychology Department, University of Amsterdam, 1972. (See Tjoa, p. 94.)

R. J. Trotter. Transcendental Meditation. Science News 104(24), 376-378 (December 15, 1973).

S. Truch. Transcendental Meditation: a boon for teachers. The Alberta Teachers' Association Magazine, May-June 1972.

R. K. Wallace. Efeitos fisiologicos da meditacao transcendental. Rev. Bras. Med. 27, 297-401 (1970).

J. White, Ed. What is Meditation? Doubleday-Anchor, New York, May 1974.a

J. White, Ed. Frontiers of Consciousness. Julian Press, New York, Spring 1974.b

J. White. Toward a Science of Consciousness. W. A. Benjamin, Inc.,
Reading, Mass., 1974. c

G. Williams, III. Transcendental Meditation: can it fight drug abuse?
Science Digest, 74-79 (February 1972).

G. Williams, III. The easiest course ever taught. Scholastic Voice,
5-8 (March 5, 1973).

R. Wolf. Mind over matter for better health. Prevention 25(1), 128-137
(January 1973).

J. Zaffarano. Transcendental Meditation: new tool of management?
Administrative Management, p. 28, May 1974.

A. Zullo. Relax with Transcendental Meditation. Marriage 55(3), 10-16
(March 1973).

EPILOGUE

by

Hans Selye, M.D., Professor and Director
Institute of Experimental Medicine and Surgery
University of Montreal
Montreal, P.Q., Canada

EPILOGUE

by

Hans Selye, M.D., Professor and Director
Institute of Experimental Medicine and Surgery
University of Montreal
Montreal, P.Q., Canada

I am pleased to furnish an "Afterword" to this valuable compila-
tion of data and references. Although I have no personal experience
in the practice of Transcendental Meditation, I have maintained an
ongoing contact with many of its proponents ever since participating
in an international symposium, under the personal direction of Maharishi
Mahesh Yogi, at Queens University. There are a number of interrelations
between the effects of TM and my own research on the medical aspects of
stress and I have long felt that a rigorous investigation of these
areas would be a most productive endeavor. This volume represents a
welcome contribution to the foundations of such an inquiry.

The primary task is to establish objectively measurable somatic
parameters for evaluating TM's influence on stress as the latter is
understood in medicine. The present review is particularly helpful in
this regard; it outlines no less than twelve physiologic correlates of
the meditative state (as compared with the states of wakefulness, sleep
and dreaming) and surveys the smaller number of psychologic studies
that have been conducted to date. The authors also deserve credit for
attempting to establish comparisons with other traditional meditational
techniques, such as Yoga and Zen.

I wish mainly to address myself to the authors' avowed goal of
"stress release," the contention that "the physiological and biochemical
changes that accompany the TM process relieve the nervous system of
strain and stresses." It is essential to point out that the medical
definition of stress does not attribute an intrinsically unpleasant or
harmful quality to stressful situations. Stress is defined as "the
nonspecific (that is, stereotyped) response of the body to any demand
made upon it." An experience of intense joy or the satisfaction of
achievement can act as a stress producer or "stressor" just as
much as anxiety or physical pain; in both cases, certain nervous and
hormonal reactions occur in essentially identical patterns.

It follows from the foregoing definition that stress is inherent in all human activity -- indeed, in life itself -- and, thus, cannot be avoided. However, it can and should be mastered. What is needed are guidelines for minimizing harmful stress (actually, distress), with its damaging accumulation of "chemical scars", while cultivating the beneficial effects of pleasant, fulfilling stress (known technically as "eustress"). Much of my own recent work has been directed towards formulating such guidelines for a biologically justifiable code of behavior.

This approach is quite compatible with the aims and principles of TM. As the current work points out, Maharishi Mahesh Yogi is opposed to the kind of meditation that induces passive introversion and indifference to the concerns of society. TM aims to produce a healthy relaxed state of mind conducive to the exercise of creative intelligence. My objective is to provide a framework for efficient and fulfilling utilization of the "pure awareness" developed by TM as part of a life with stress, but without distress.

To this end, I have proposed[1] that the biblical exhortation to "Love thy neighbor as thyself" be reformulated to read; "Earn thy neighbor's love." The traditional admonition is biologically unrealistic since, for example, the survival of big fish depends on their eating smaller fish. My suggested rewording takes into account the natural egotism inherent in man and attempts to transform it into altruistic behavior. It does so by redirecting the selfish hoarding instinct towards the accumulation of the most valuable human possession: the love, respect and goodwill of others. Thus, it deprives potential enemies of motivation for aggression and thereby enhances our sense of security.

Four decades of laboratory observation and reflection have convinced me that only such "altruistic egotism" can act as a framework of any biologically grounded scientific code of human behavior. The evolution of diverse species depended largely on the development of processes permitting many cells to live in harmony with a minimum of stress between them, serving their own best interests by insuring the survival of the entire complex structure. There later developed collaboration among individuals of the same and even of different species. For human beings and societies coping fitfully with the stress of living together, the achievement of such an orderly and disciplined mutual cooperation is an urgent priority.

146

I feel confident that "The Psychobiology of Transcendental Meditation: A Literature Review" will furnish a most useful basis for a scientific approach to this problem.

Montréal, Québec
24 May 1974

---

[1]
Stress Without Distress.   J.B. Lippincott Company, New York--Philadelphia (1974).

SUBJECT INDEX

AUTHOR INDEX